worship BAND PLAY-ALONG

GUITAR EDITION *Volume 2*

Here I Am to Worship

Recorded and produced by Jim Reith at BeatHouse Music, Milwaukee, WI

Lead Vocals by Tonia Emrich and Jim Reith
Background Vocals by Jim Reith, Janna Wolf and Joy Palisoc Bach
Guitars by Mike DeRose and Joe Gorman
Bass by Chris Kringel
Keyboard by Kurt Cowling
Drums by Del Bennett

ISBN 978-1-4234-1718-7

HAL•LEONARD®
CORPORATION
7777 W. BLUEMOUND RD. P.O. BOX 13819 MILWAUKEE, WI 53213

Visit Hal Leonard Online at
www.halleonard.com

Come, Now Is the Time to Worship

Words and Music by Brian Doerksen

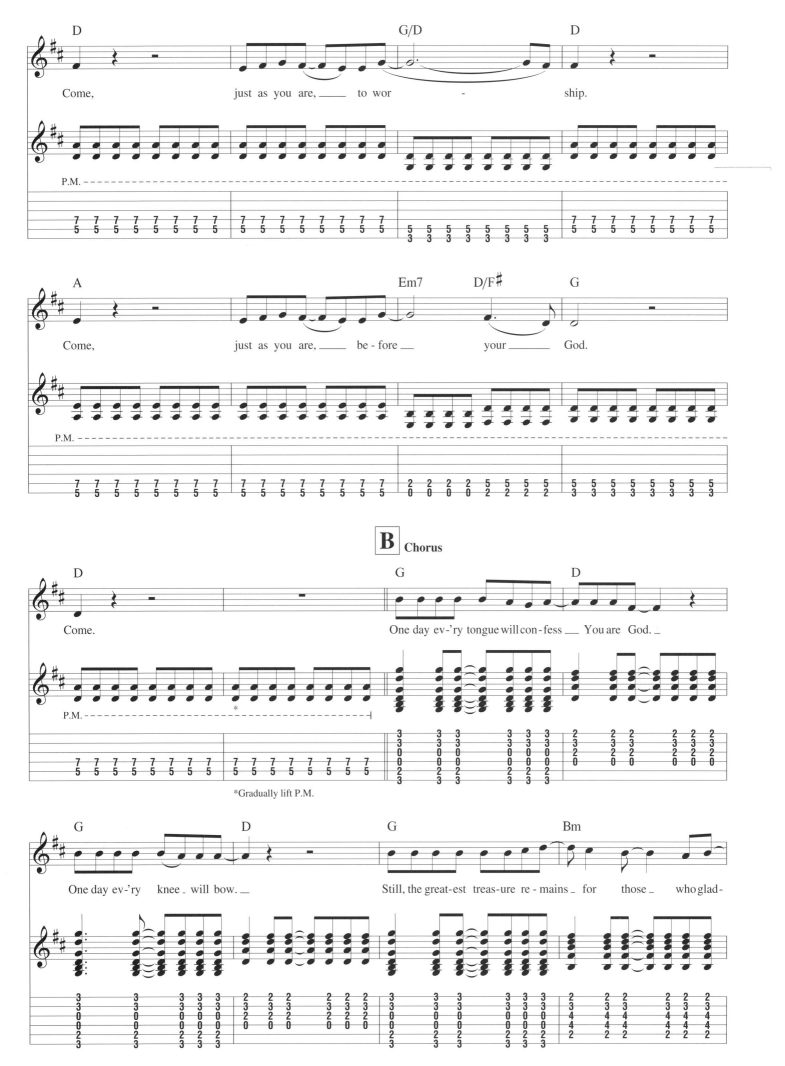

3

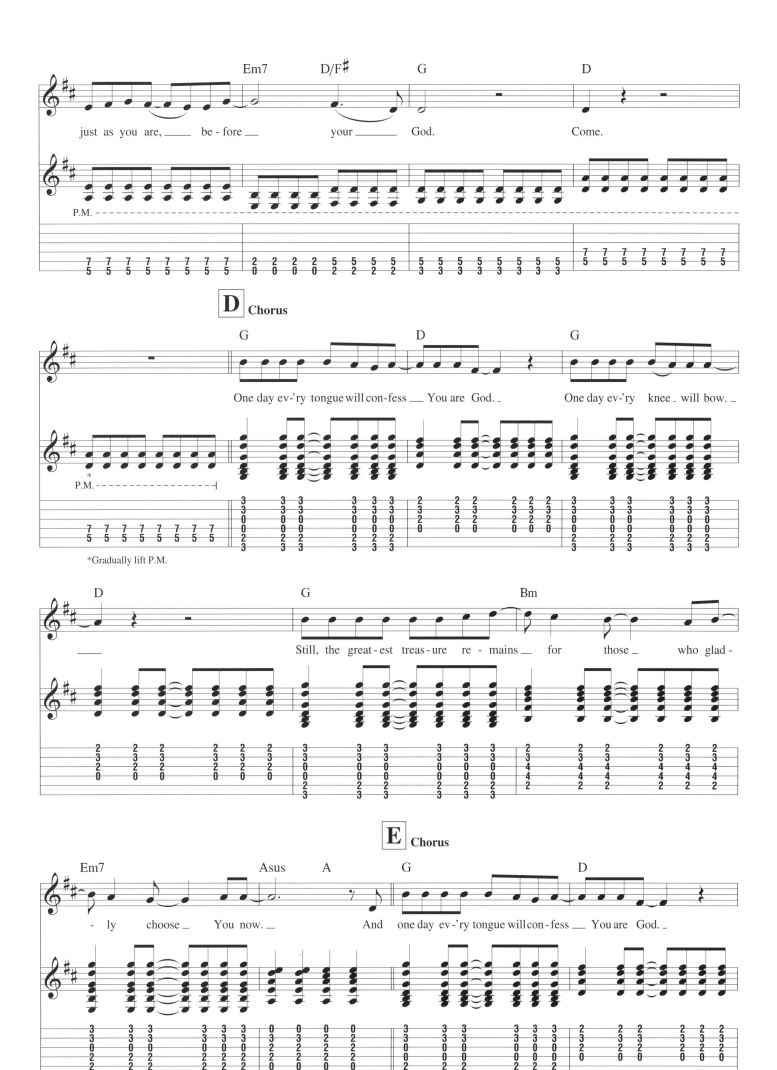

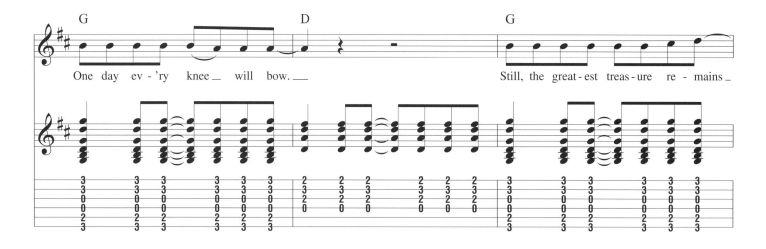

One day ev-'ry knee _ will bow. _ Still, the great-est treas-ure re - mains _

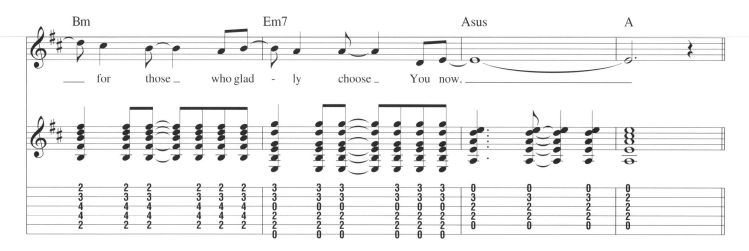

_ for those _ who glad - ly choose _ You now. ____

F **Verse**

Come, now is the time _ to wor -

ship. Come, now is the time _ to give _ your ____

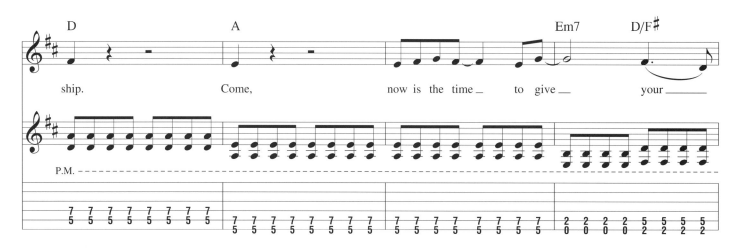

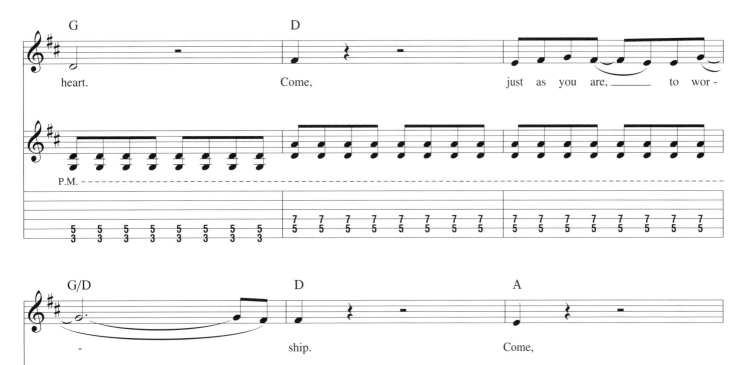

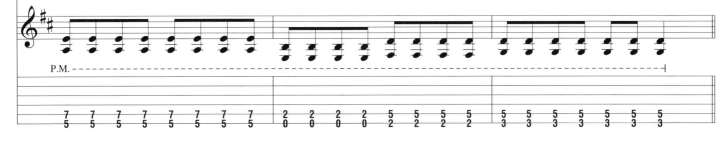

Outro

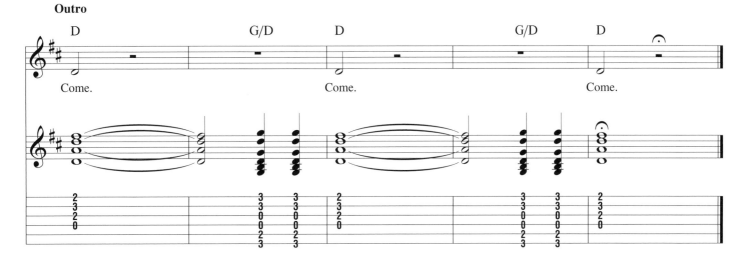

Give Us Clean Hands

Words and Music by Charlie Hall

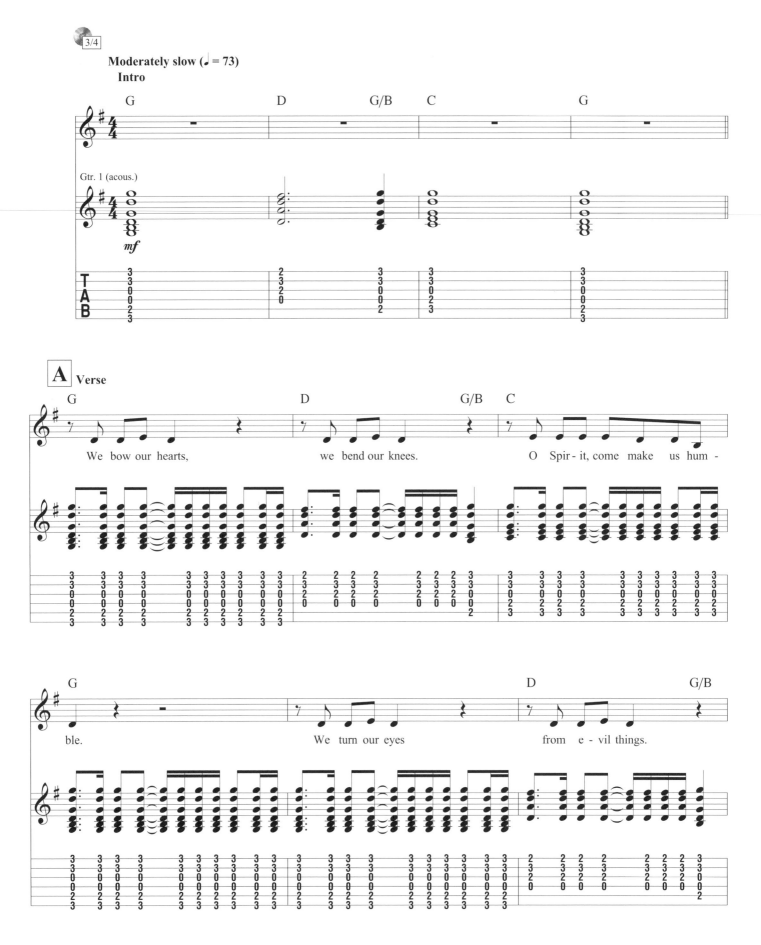

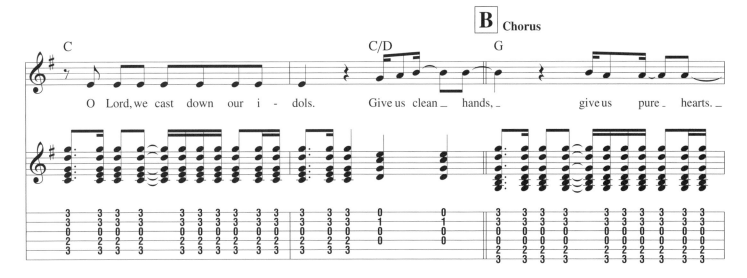

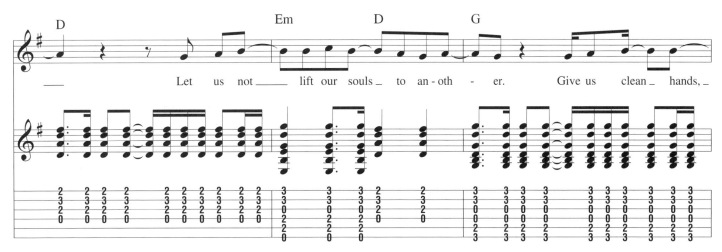

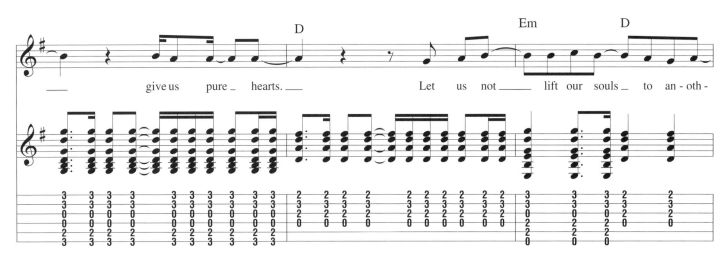

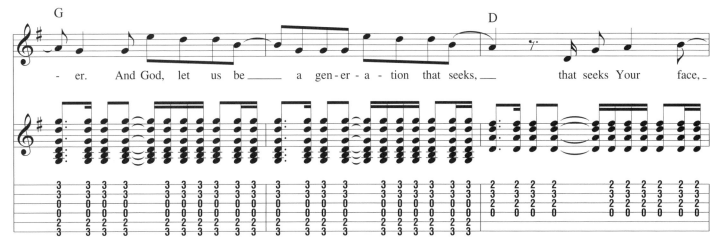

9

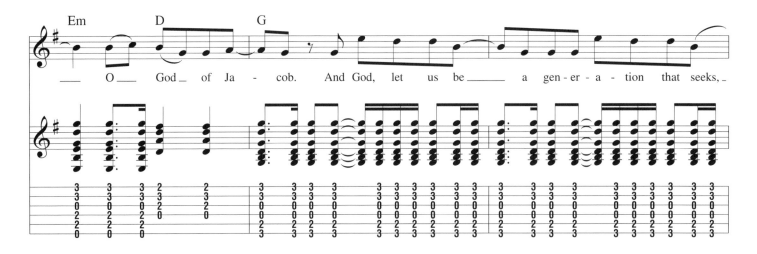

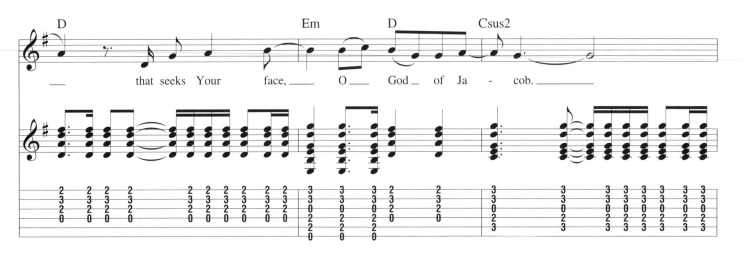

C Verse

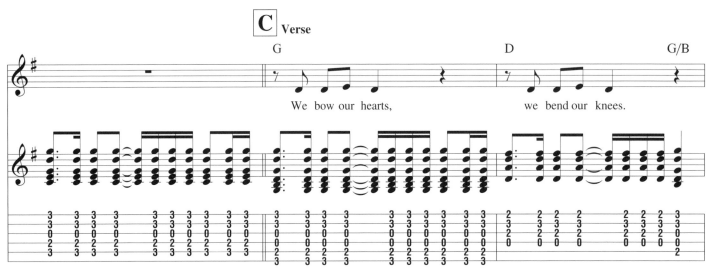

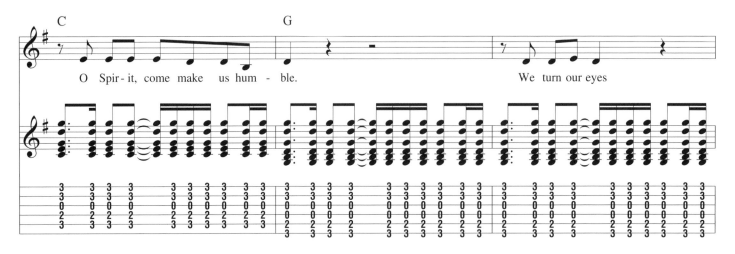

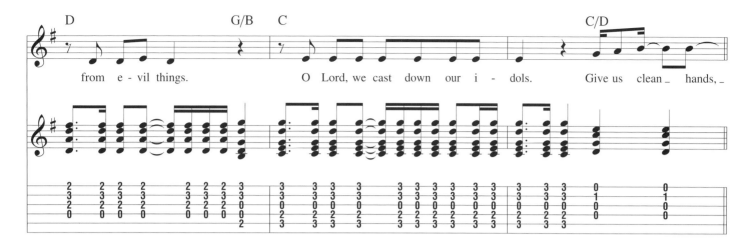

from e - vil things. O Lord, we cast down our i - dols. Give us clean _ hands, _

D Chorus

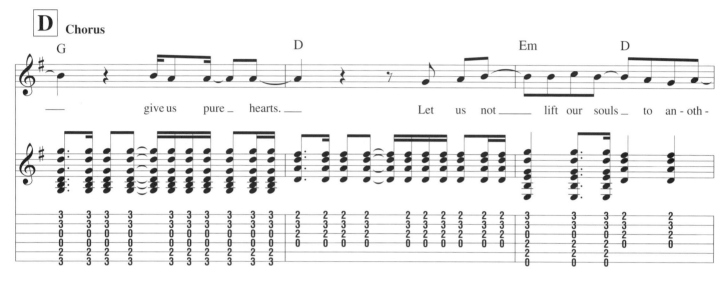

_ give us pure _ hearts. _ Let us not _____ lift our souls _ to an - oth -

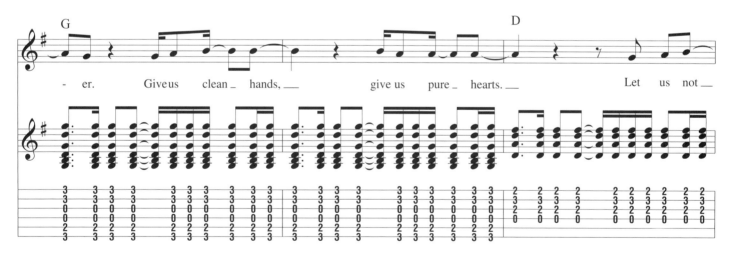

- er. Give us clean _ hands, _____ give us pure _ hearts. _ Let us not _

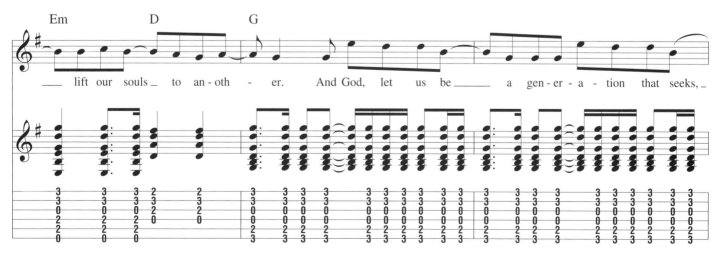

_ lift our souls _ to an - oth - er. And God, let us be _____ a gen - er - a - tion that seeks, _

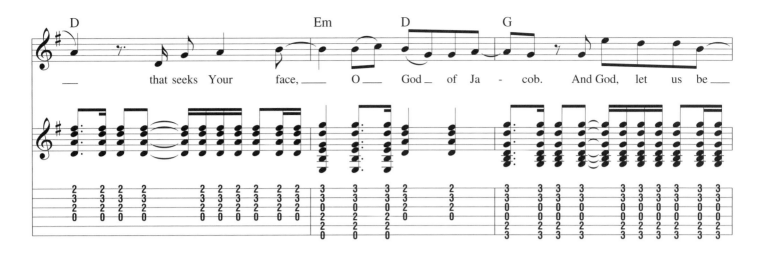

that seeks Your face, ___ O ___ God ___ of Ja - cob. And God, let us be ___

___ a gen - er - a - tion that seeks, ___ that seeks Your face, ___ O ___ God ___ of Ja -

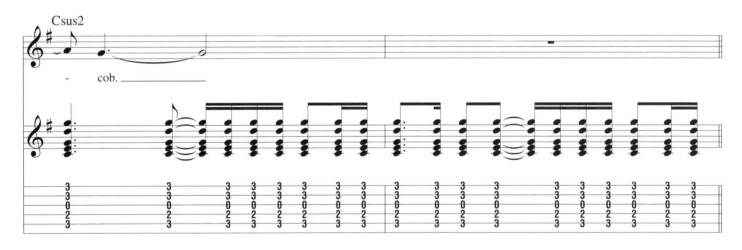

- cob. ___

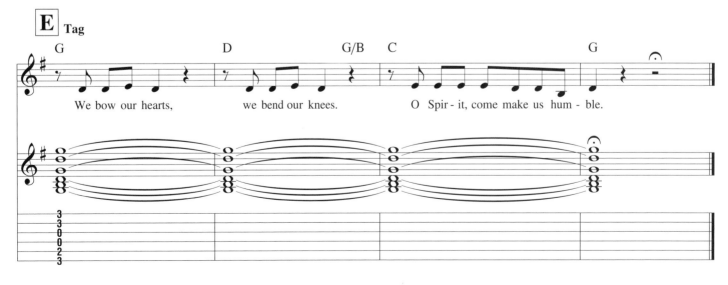

We bow our hearts, we bend our knees. O Spir - it, come make us hum - ble.

Hear Our Praises

Words and Music by Reuben Morgan

5/6

Moderately fast (♩ = 125)
Intro

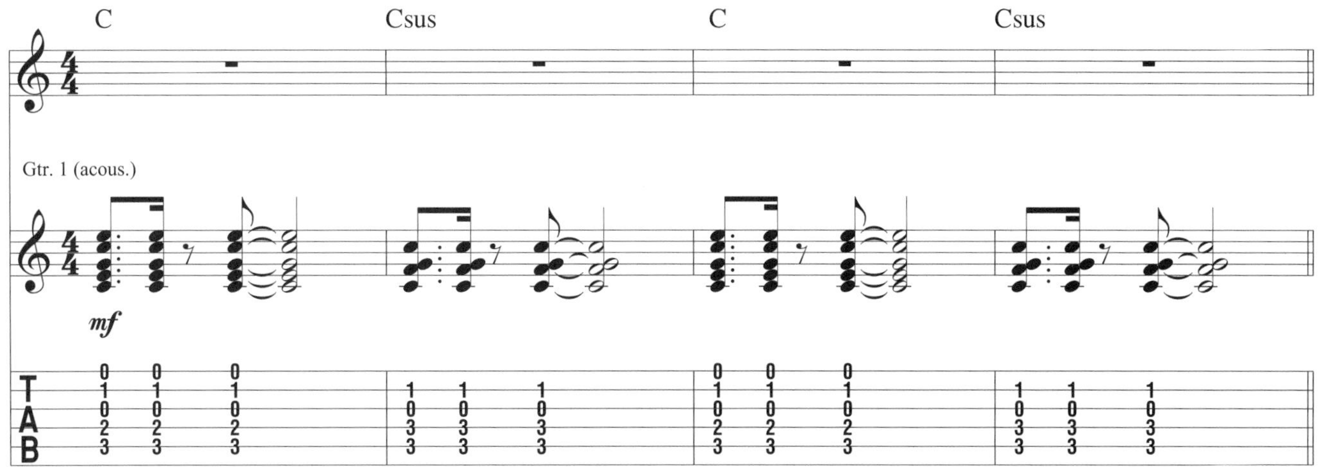

C
Csus
C
Csus
Gtr. 1 (acous.)
mf
T
A
B
0 0 0 1 1 1 0 0 0 1 1 1 0 0 0 1 1 1
0 1 0 2 3
1 0 3 3
0 1 0 2 3
1 0 3 3

A Verse 1

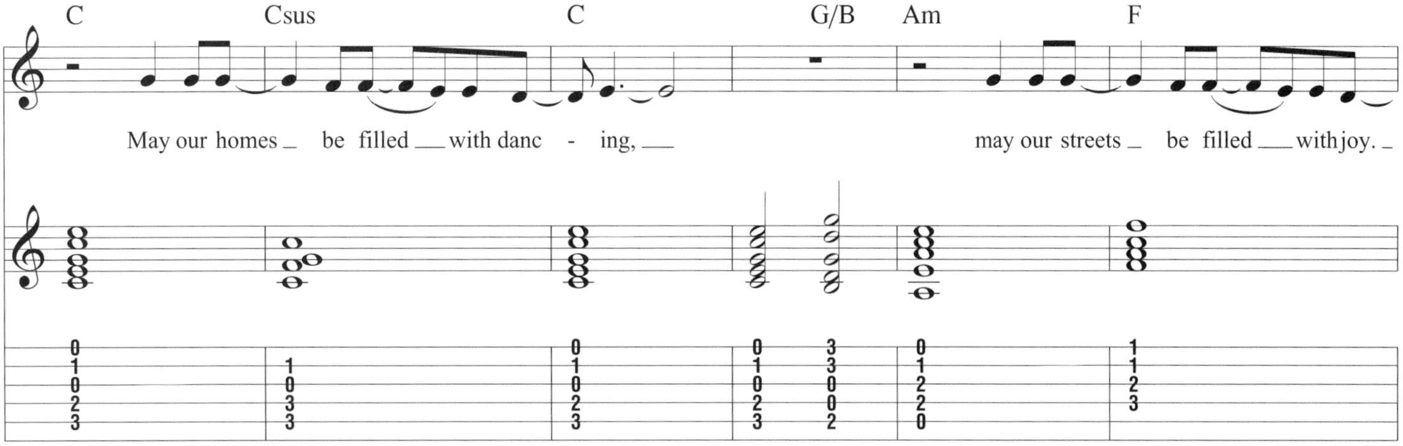

C
Csus
C
G/B
Am
F
May our homes be filled with danc - ing,
may our streets be filled with joy.
0 1 0 2 3
1 0 3 3
0 1 0 2 3
0 1 0 2 3
3 3 0 0 2
0 1 2 2 0
1 1 2 3

Gsus
G
C
Csus
C
G/B
May in - jus - tice bow to Je - sus
3 1 0 0 2 3
3 0 0 0 2 3
0 1 0 2 3
1 0 3 3
0 1 0 2 3
0 1 0 2 3
3 3 0 0 2

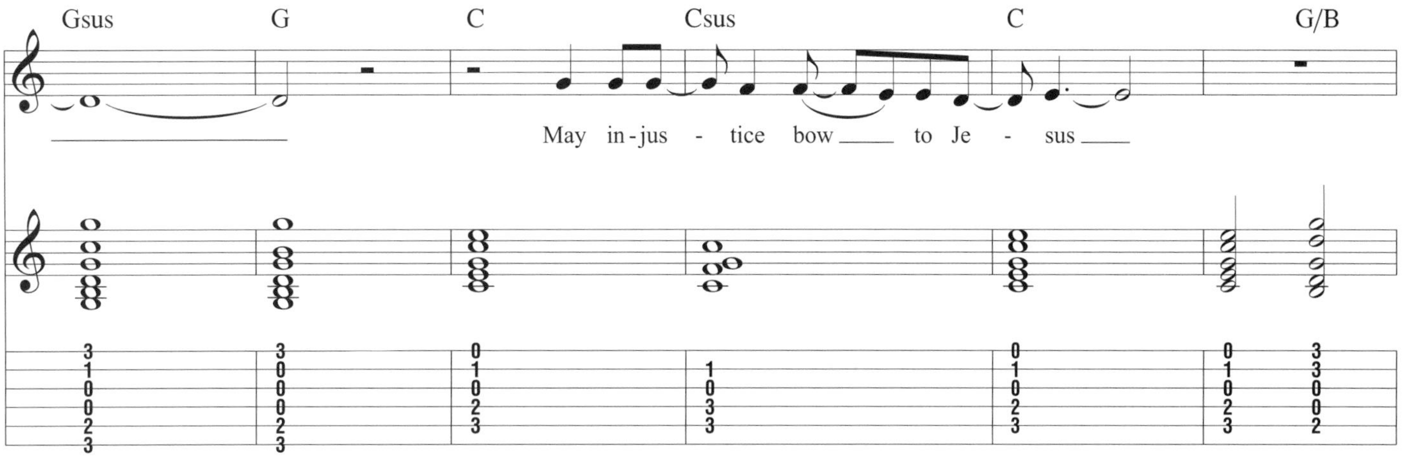

as the peo - ple turn ___ to pray. ___ From the moun - tain ___

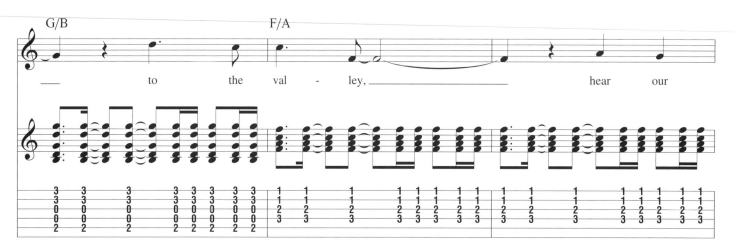

___ to the val - ley, ___ hear our

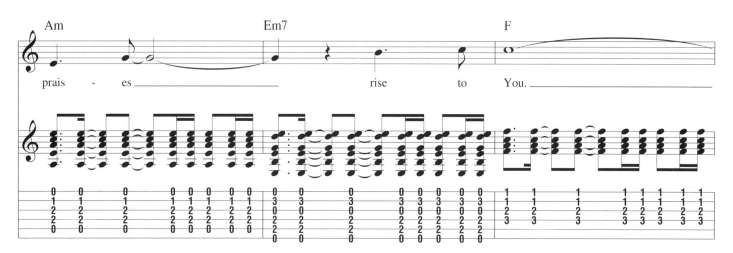

prais - es ___ rise to You. ___

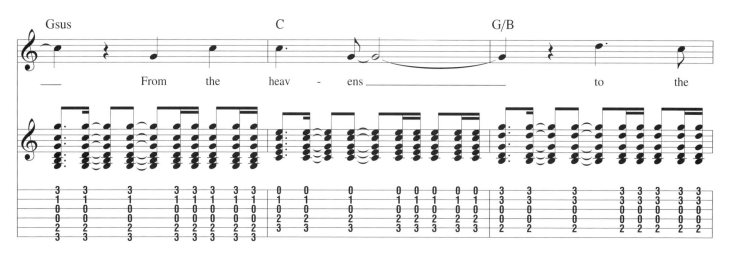

___ From the heav - ens ___ to the

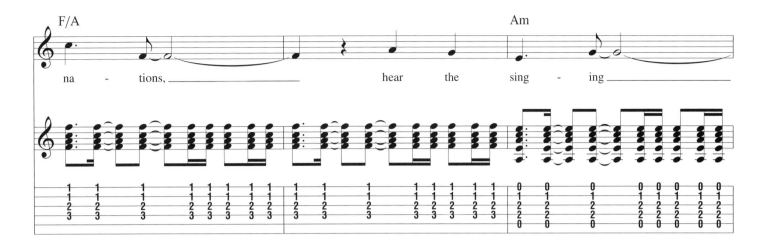

na - tions,_____ hear the sing - ing _____

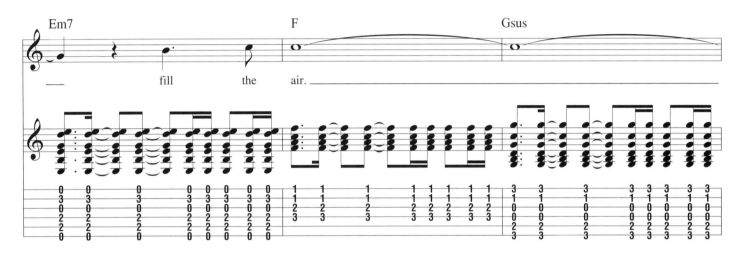

___ fill the air. _____

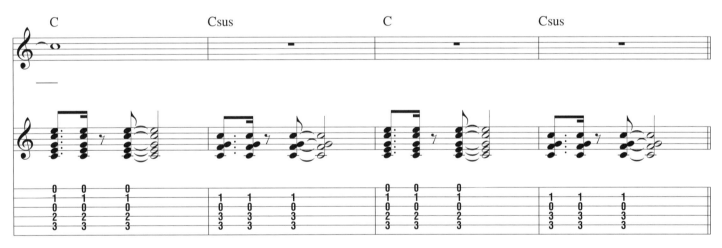

C **Verse 2**

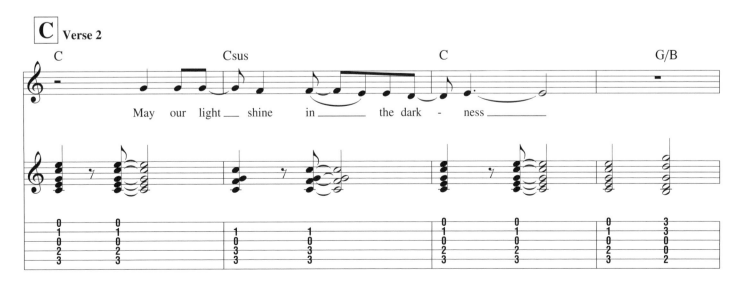

May our light ___ shine in ___ the dark - ness ___

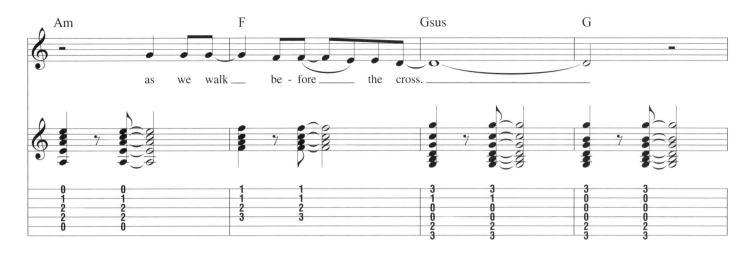

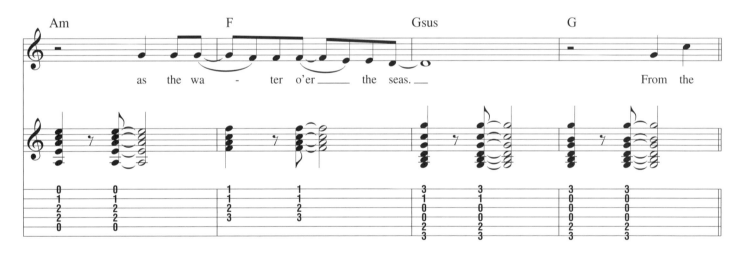

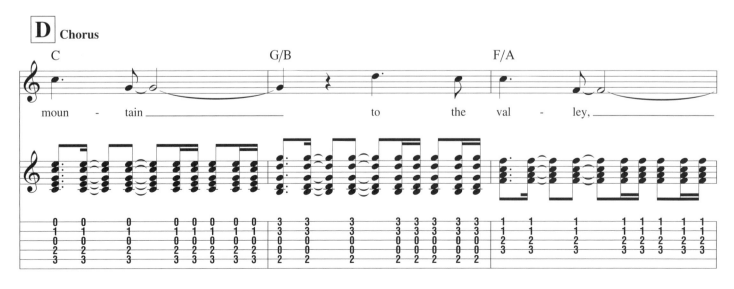

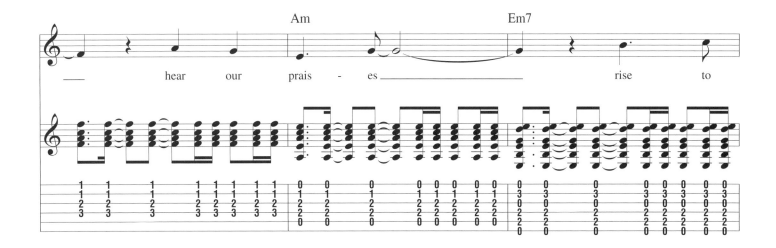

hear our prais - es _____ rise to

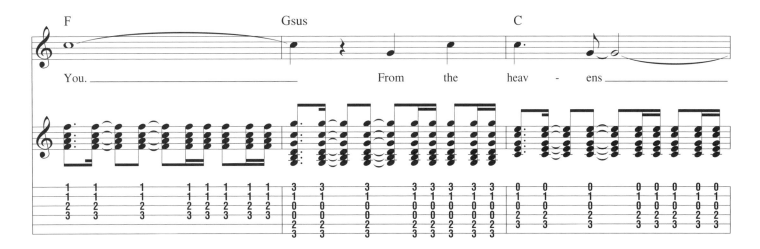

You. _____ From the heav - ens _____

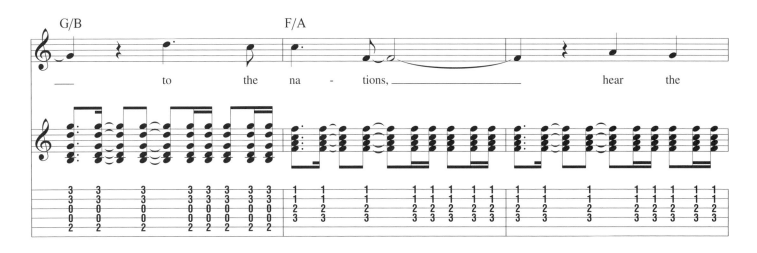

___ to the na - tions, _____ hear the

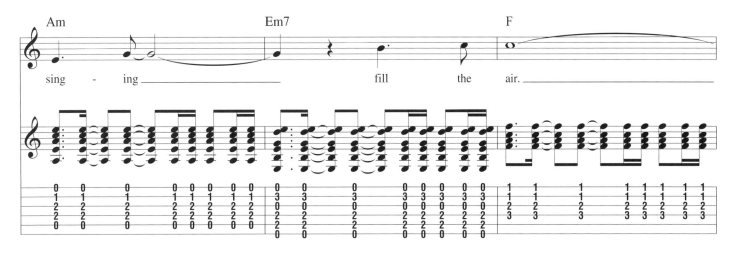

sing - ing _____ fill the air. _____

Chorus

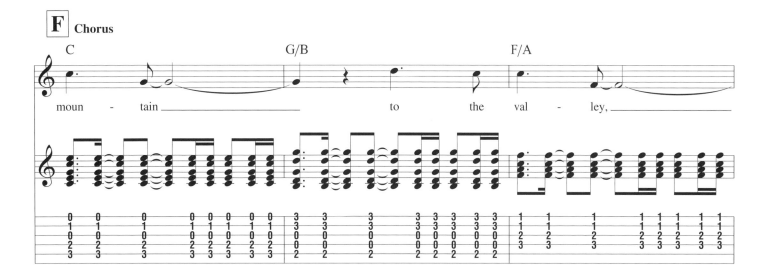

moun - tain _____ to the val - ley, _____

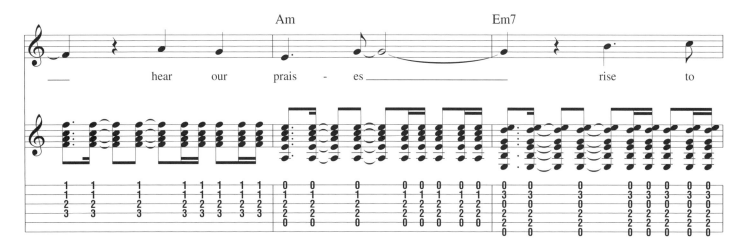

___ hear our prais - es _____ rise to

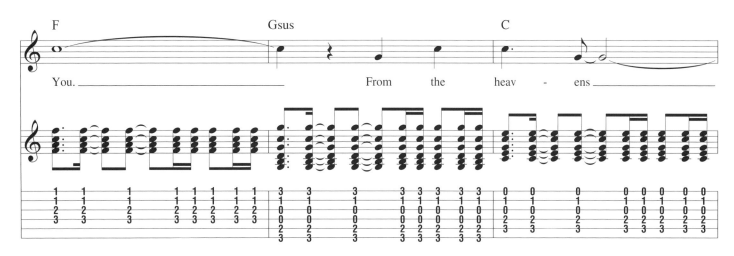

You. _____ From the heav - ens _____

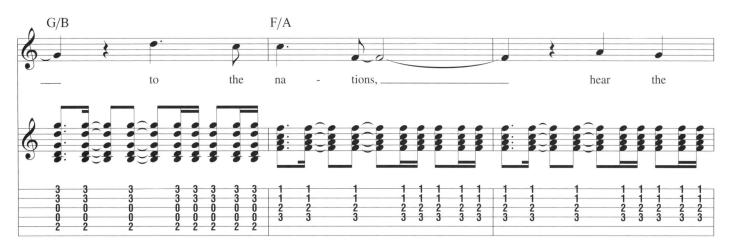

___ to the na - tions, _____ hear the

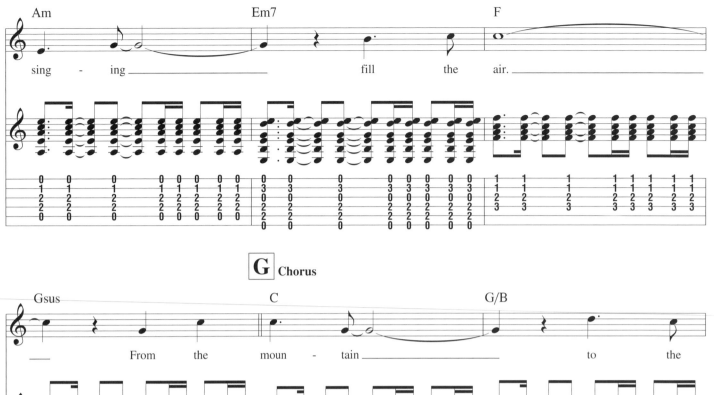

sing - ing _____ fill the air. _____

G Chorus

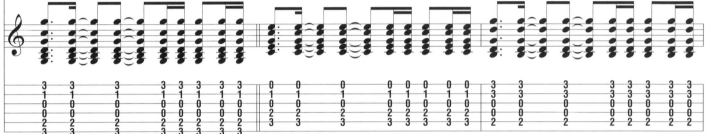

_____ From the moun - tain _____ to the

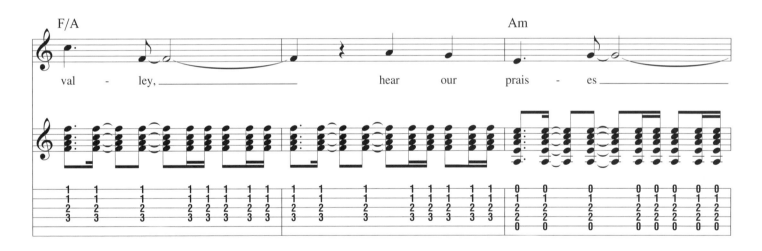

val - ley, _____ hear our prais - es _____

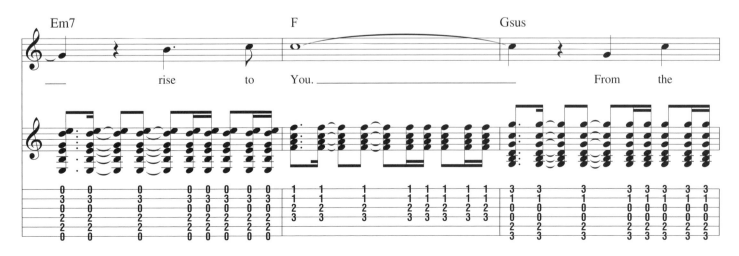

_____ rise to You. _____ From the

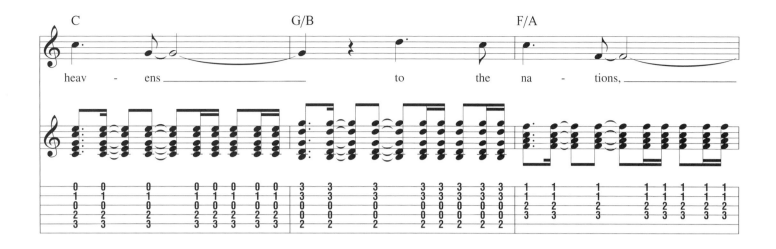

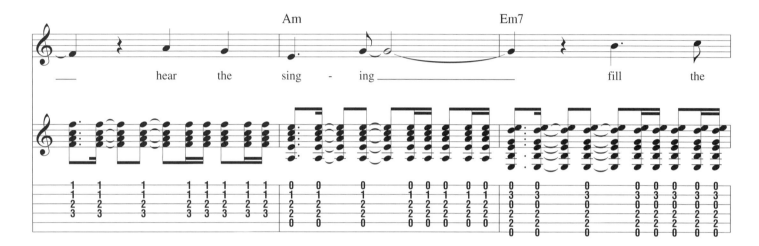

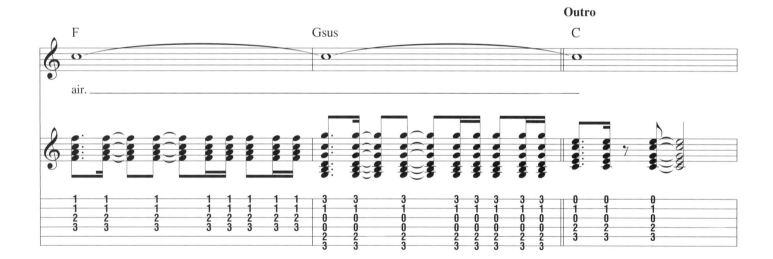

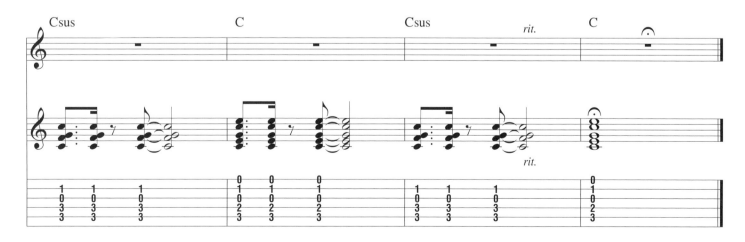

Here I Am to Worship

Words and Music by Tim Hughes

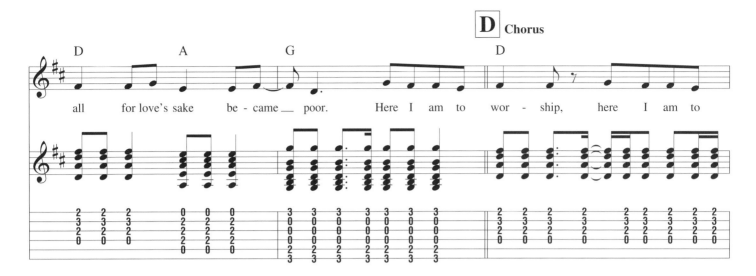

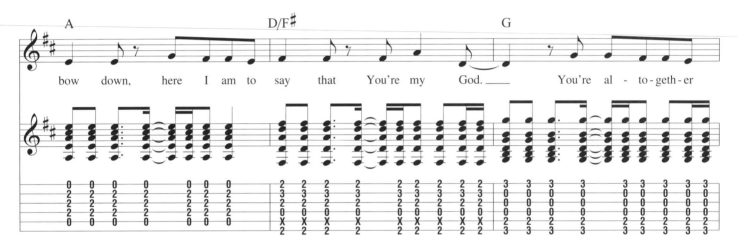

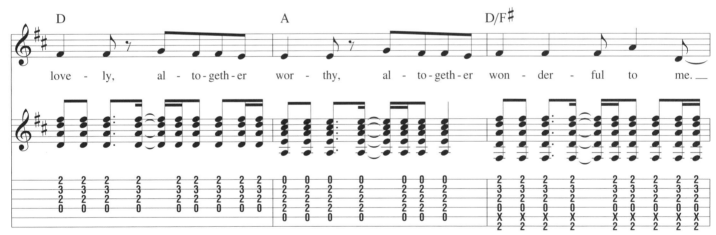

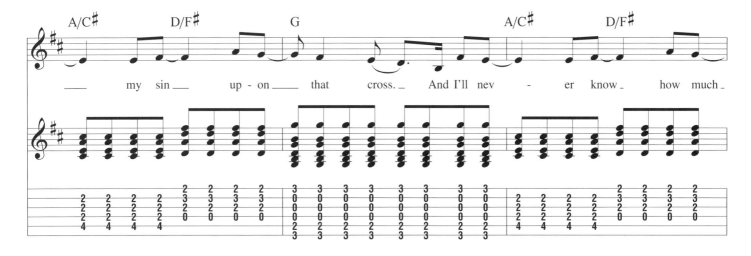

my sin __ up-on __ that cross. __ And I'll nev - er know __ how much __

it cost __ to see __ my sin __ up-on __ that cross. __

F Chorus

And here I am to wor - ship, here I am to bow down, here I am to

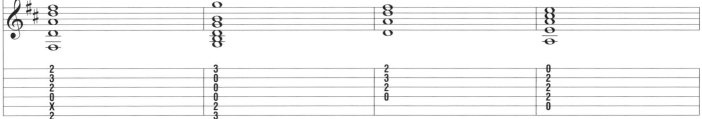

say that You're my God. __ You're al - to-geth-er love - ly, al - to-geth-er wor - thy, al - to-geth-er

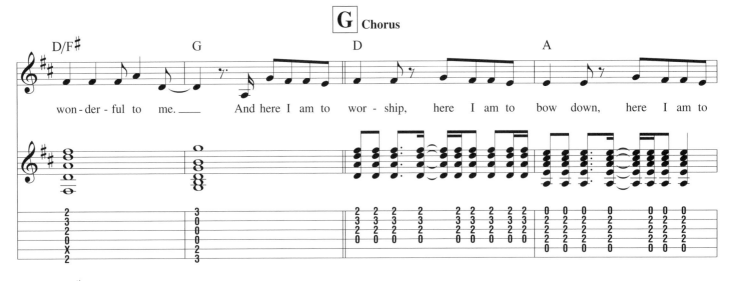

G Chorus

won-der-ful to me. ___ And here I am to wor-ship, here I am to bow down, here I am to

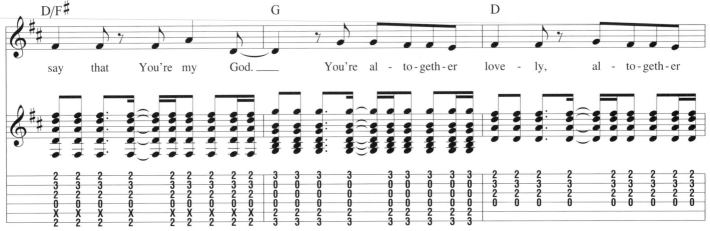

say that You're my God. ___ You're al-to-geth-er love-ly, al-to-geth-er

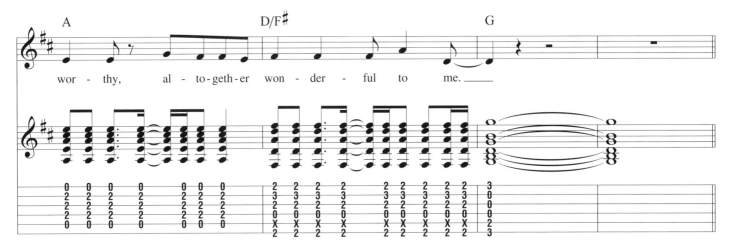

wor-thy, al-to-geth-er won-der-ful to me. ___

H Tag

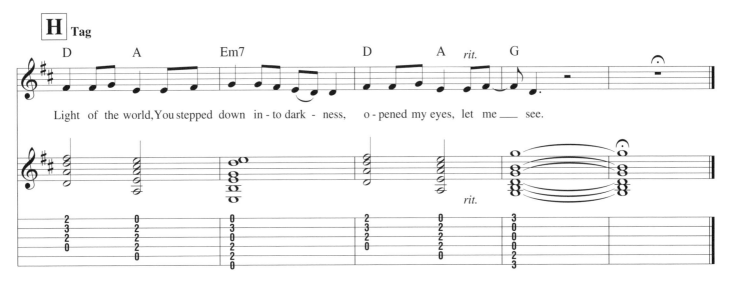

Light of the world, You stepped down in-to dark-ness, o-pened my eyes, let me ___ see.

You're Worthy of My Praise

Words and Music by David Ruis

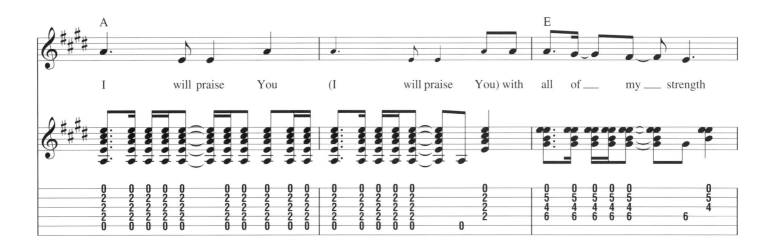

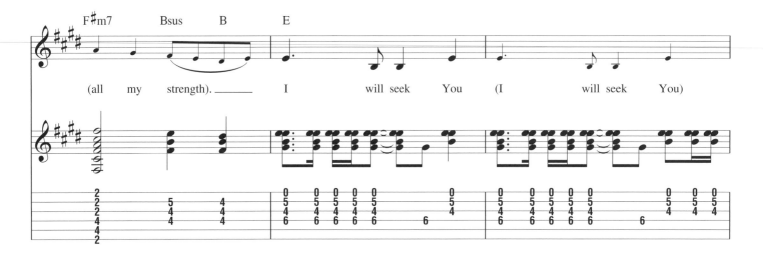

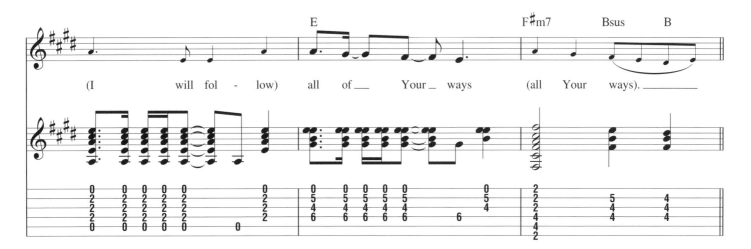

B Chorus

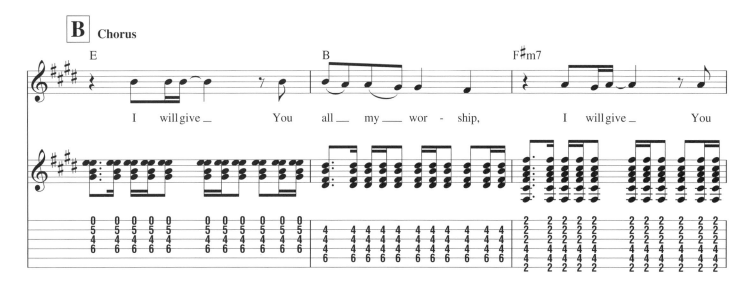

I will give _ You all _ my _ wor - ship, I will give _ You

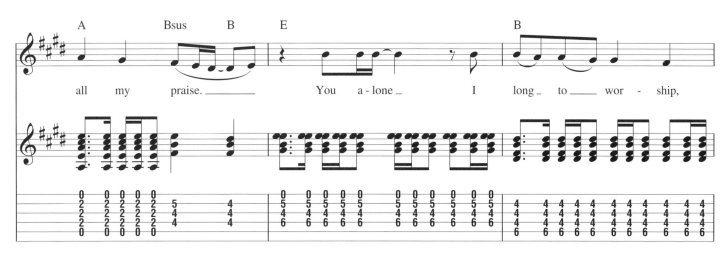

all my praise. _____ You a - lone _ I long _ to ____ wor - ship,

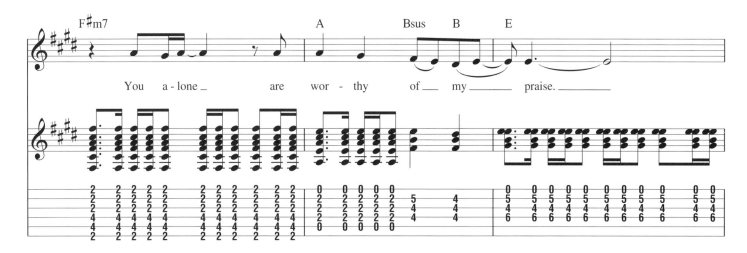

You a - lone _ are wor - thy of _ my _____ praise. _____

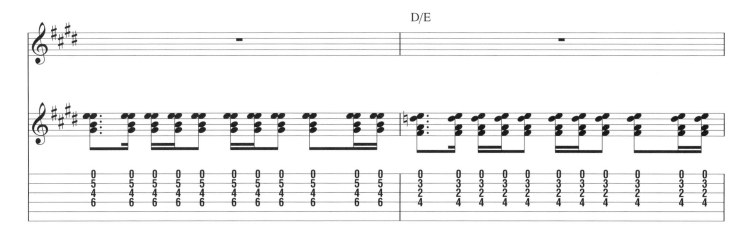

C Verse 2

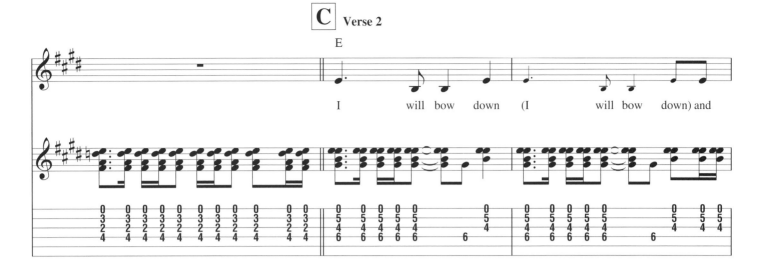

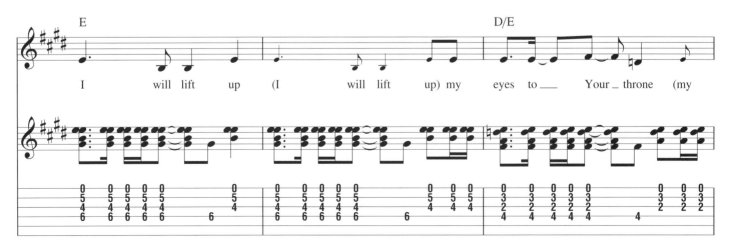

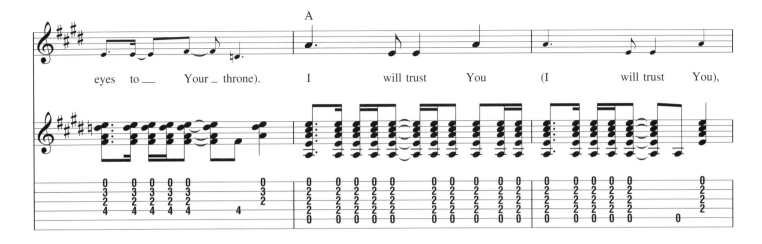

eyes to __ Your __ throne). I will trust You (I will trust You),

D Chorus

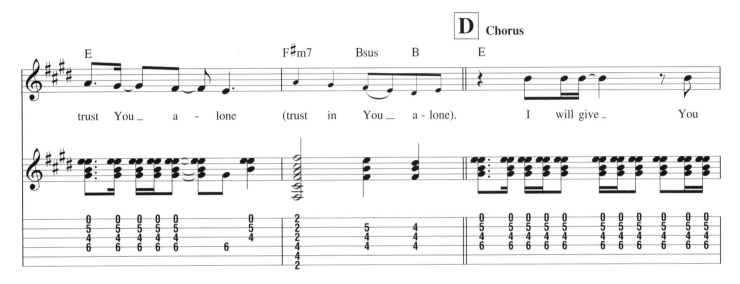

trust You __ a - lone (trust in You __ a - lone). I will give __ You

all __ my __ wor - ship, I will give __ You all my praise. __

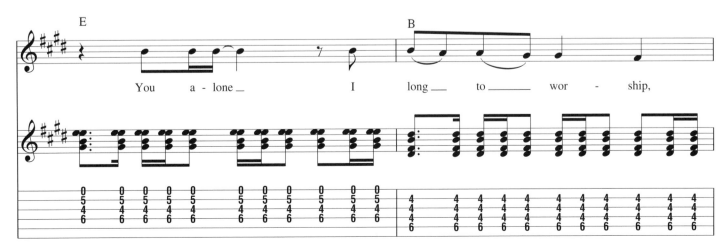

You a - lone __ I long __ to __ wor - ship,

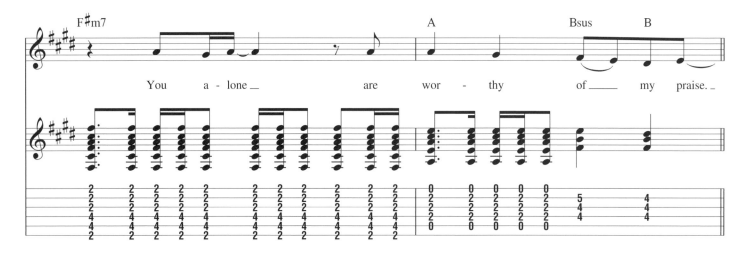

You a - lone ___ are wor - thy of ___ my praise. ___

E Chorus

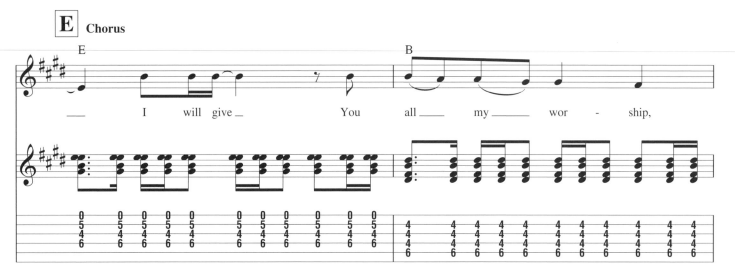

___ I will give ___ You all ___ my ___ wor - ship,

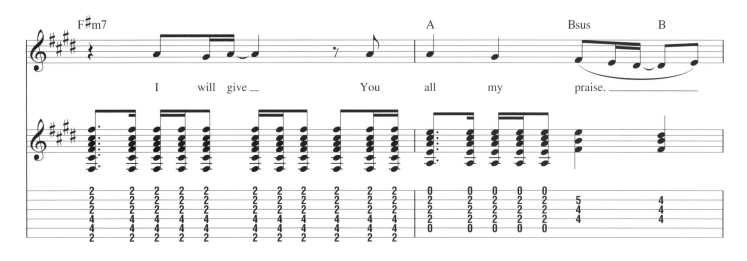

I will give ___ You all my praise. ___

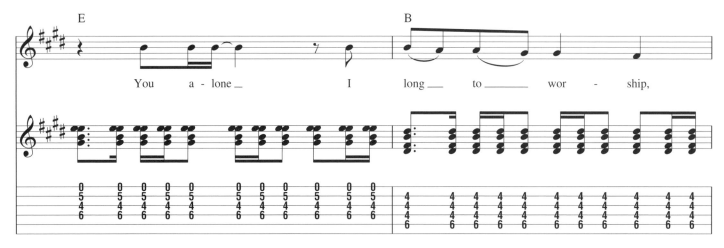

You a - lone ___ I long ___ to ___ wor - ship,

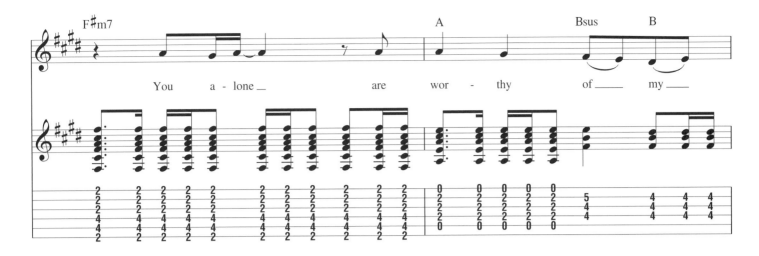

You a-lone___ are wor-thy of ___ my ___

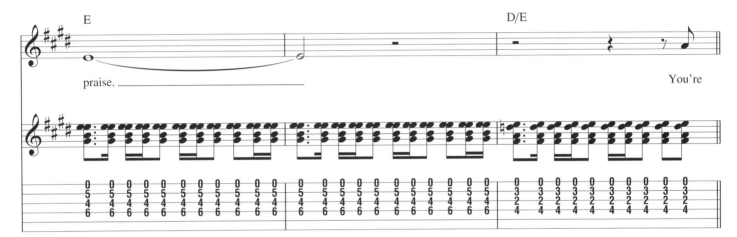

praise. ___

You're

F Tag

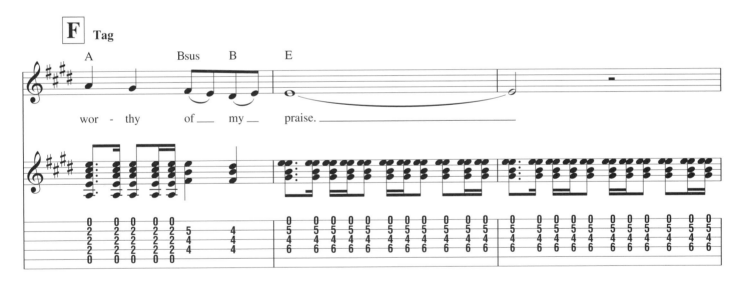

wor-thy of ___ my ___ praise. ___

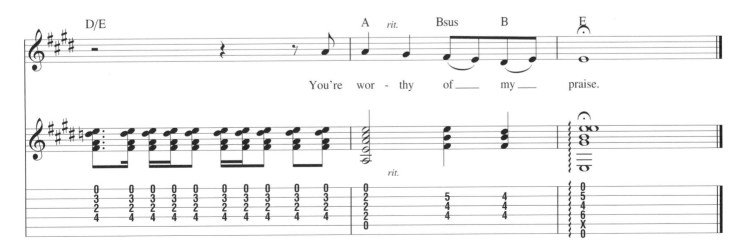

You're wor-thy of ___ my ___ praise.

33

I Give You My Heart

Words and Music by Reuben Morgan

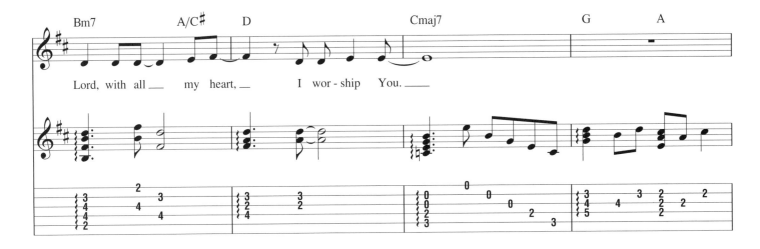

Lord, with all ____ my heart, ____ I wor-ship You. ____

All I have _ with-in _____ me, I give You praise. _

All that I ____ a - dore ____ is in You. ____

B **Chorus**

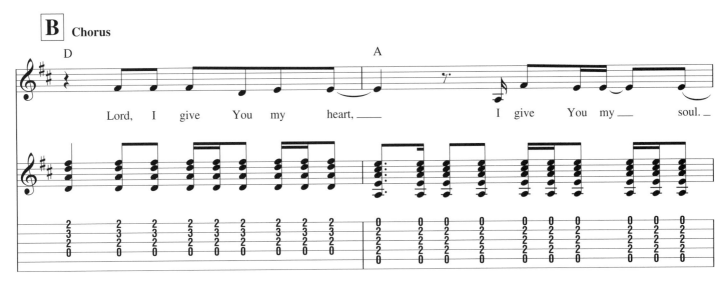

Lord, I give You my heart, ____ I give You my ____ soul. _

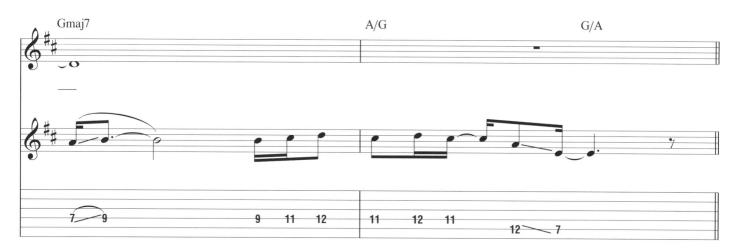

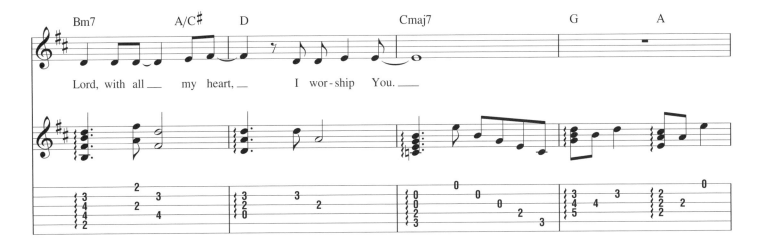

D Chorus

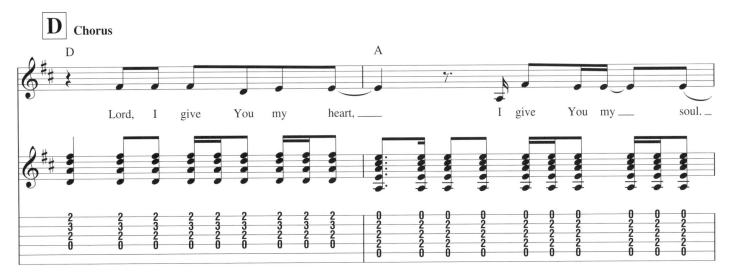

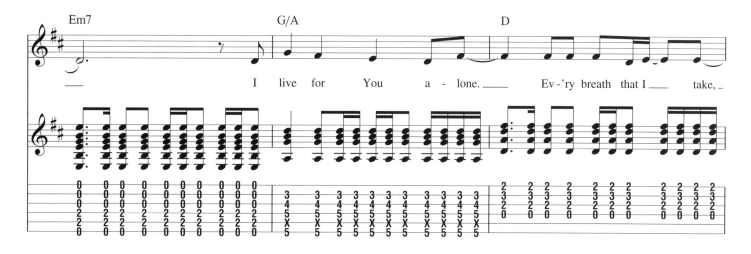

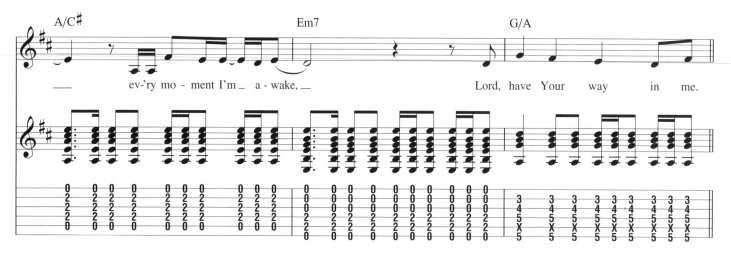

E Chorus

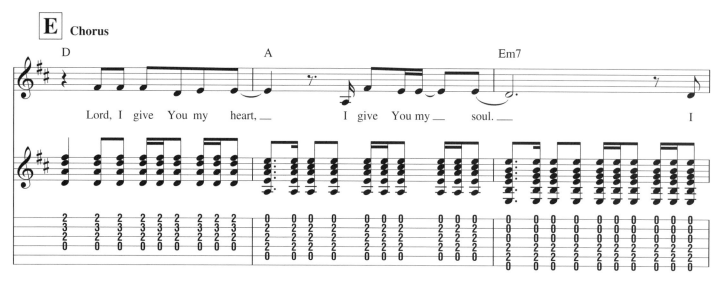

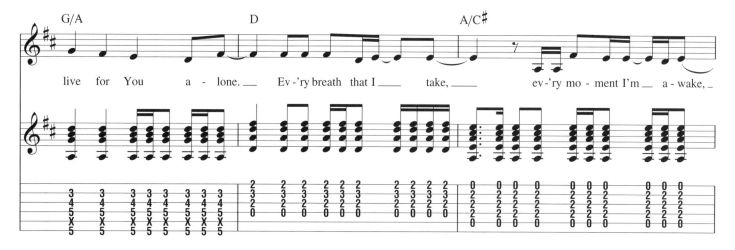

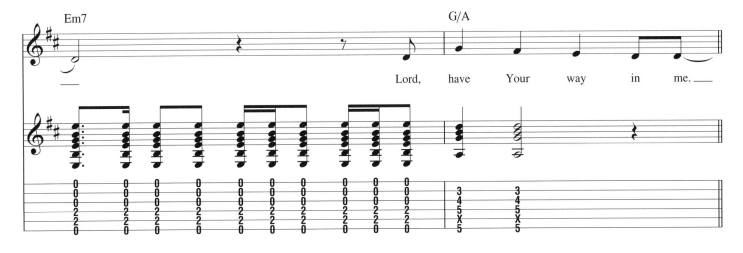

Lord, have Your way in me. ___

F **Outro**

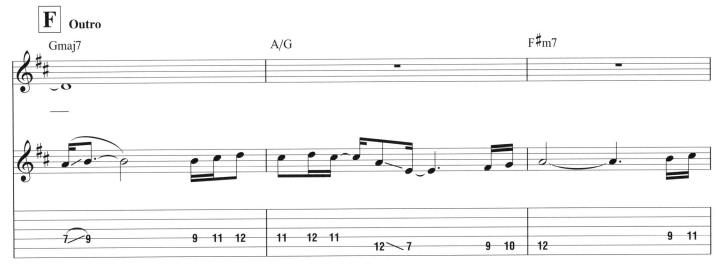

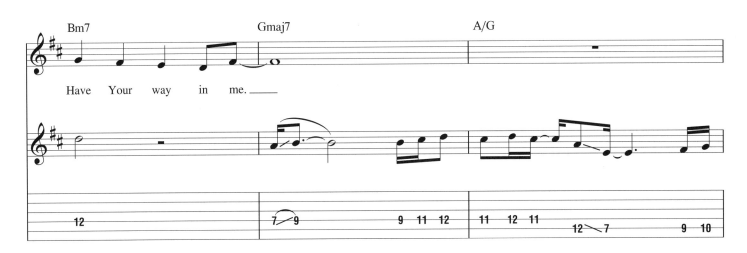

Have Your way in me. ___

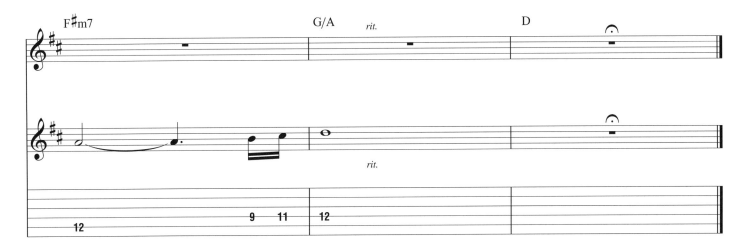

Let Everything That Has Breath

Words and Music by Matt Redman

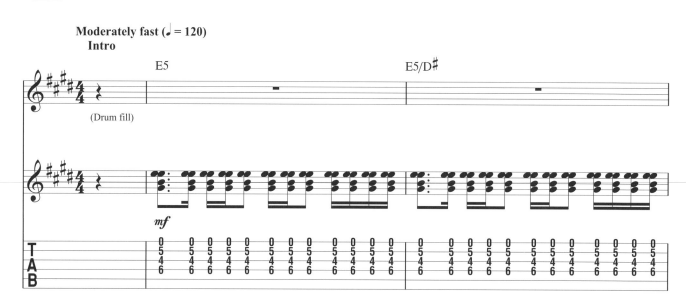

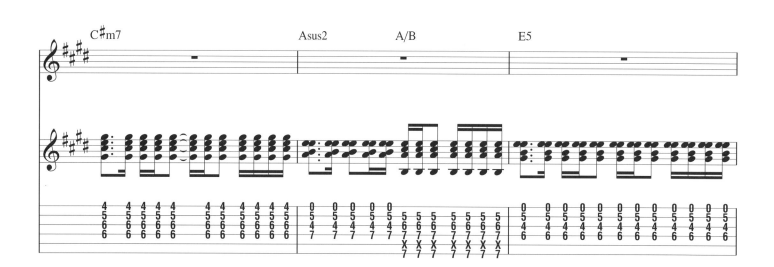

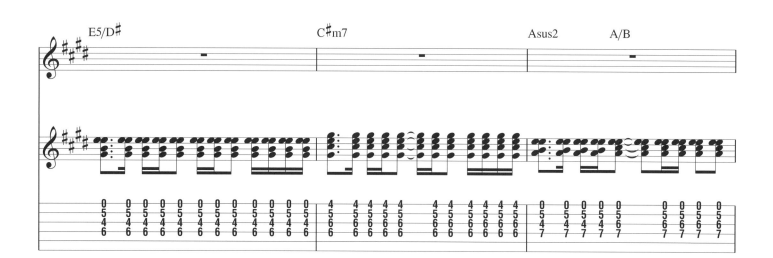

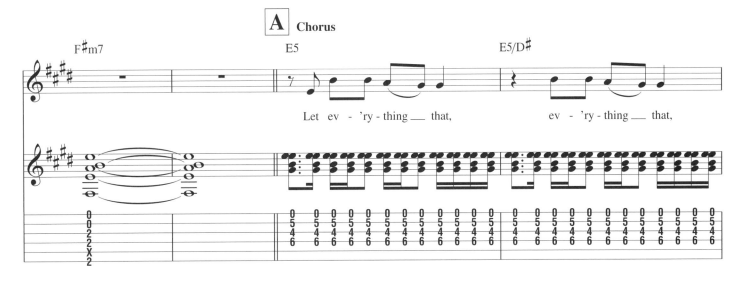

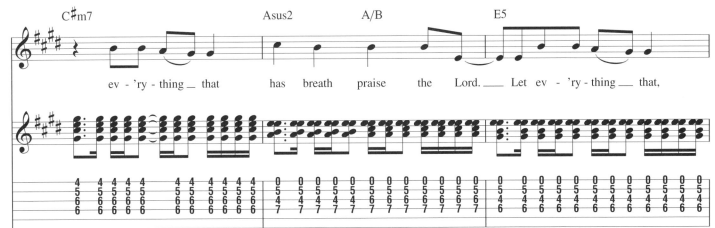

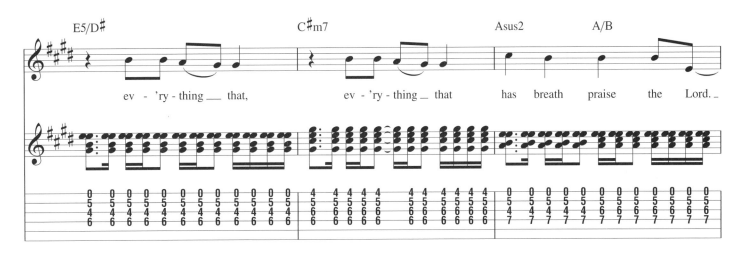

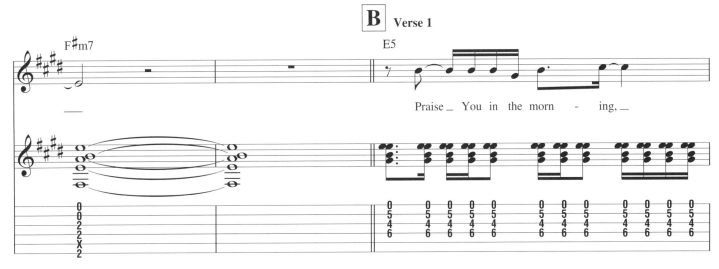

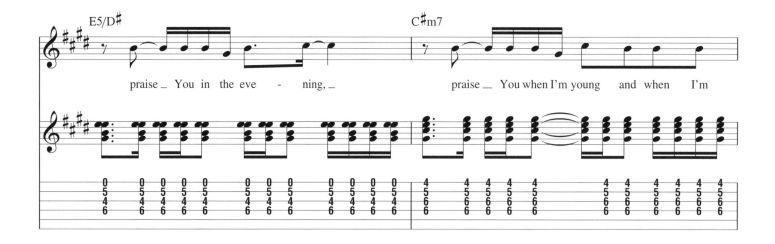

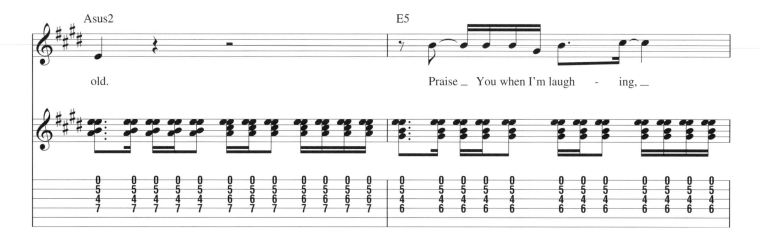

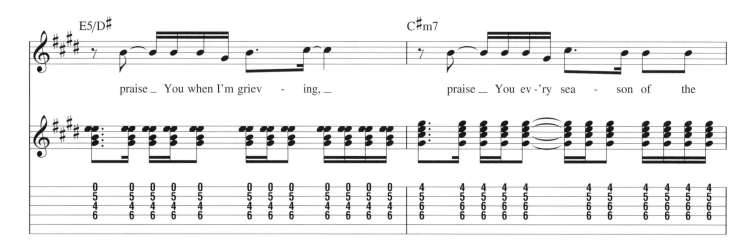

C **Pre-Chorus 1**

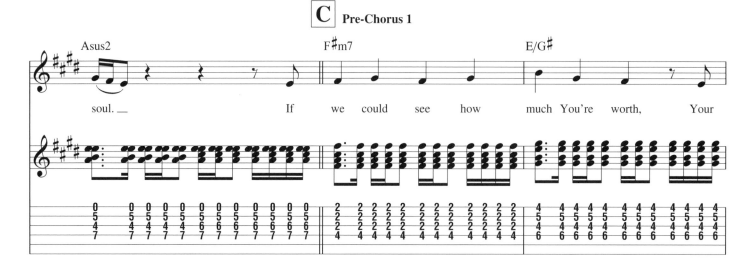

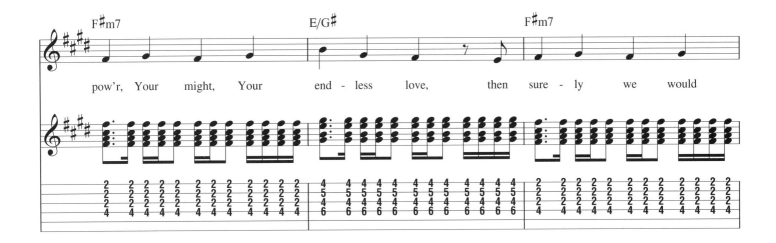

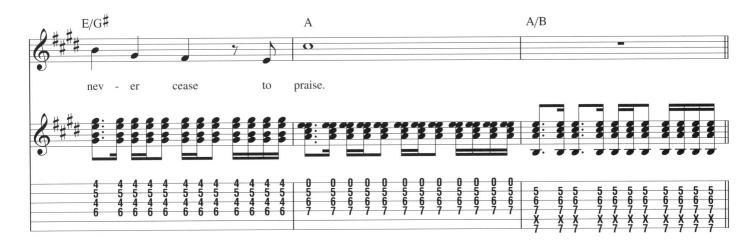

D Chorus

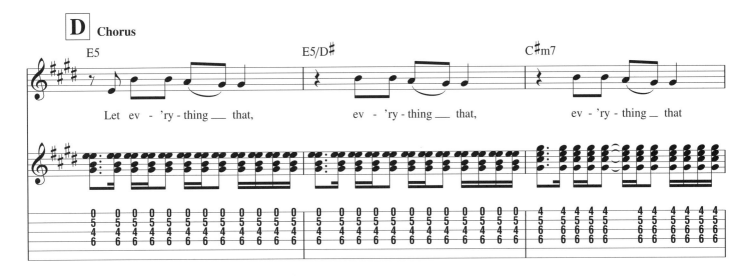

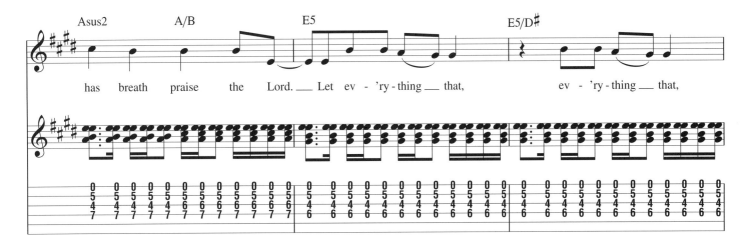

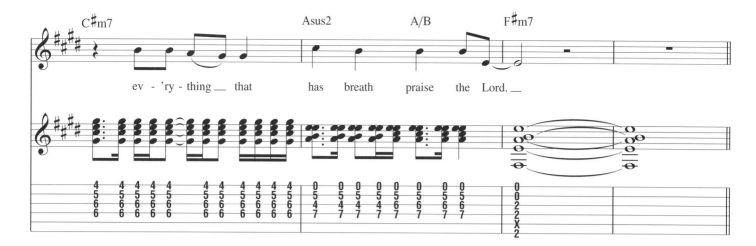

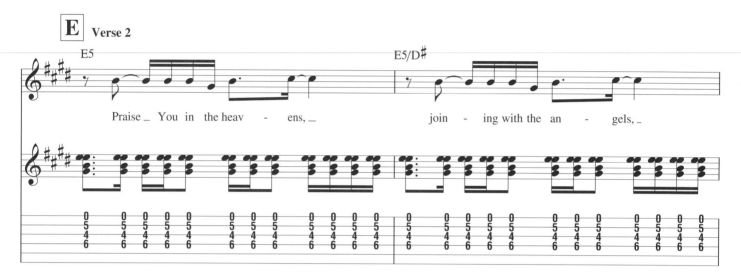

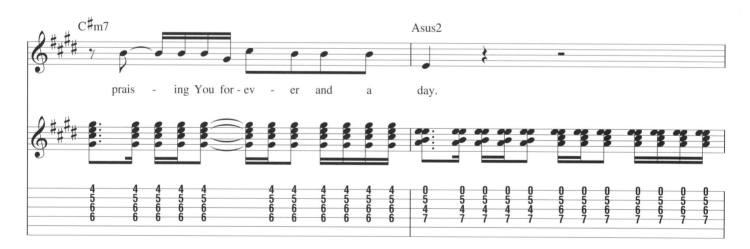

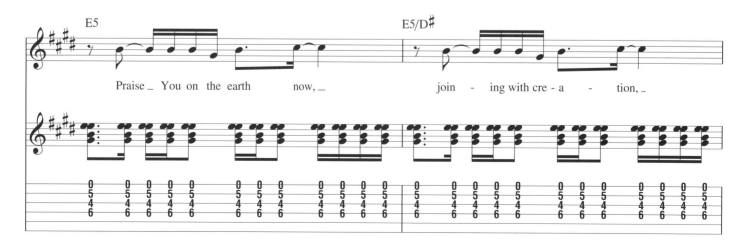

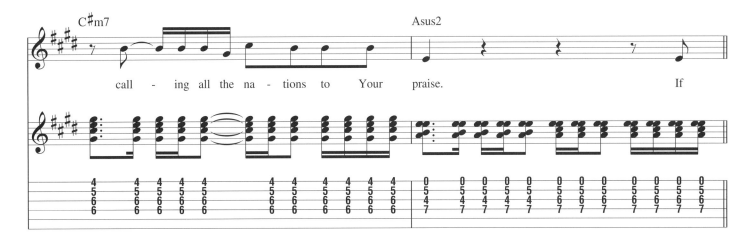

call - ing all the na - tions to Your praise. If

F Pre-Chorus 2

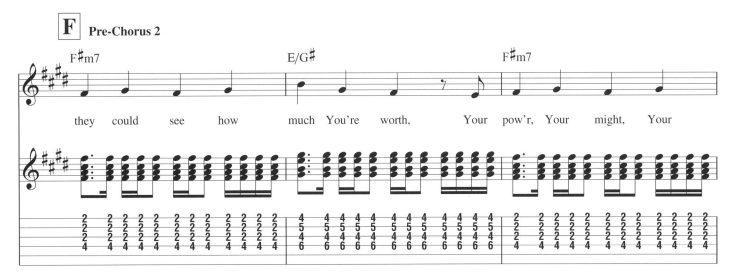

they could see how much You're worth, Your pow'r, Your might, Your

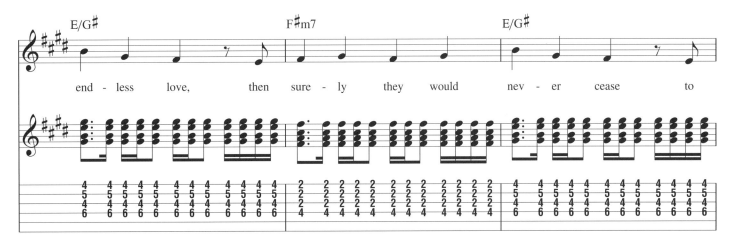

end - less love, then sure - ly they would nev - er cease to

G Chorus

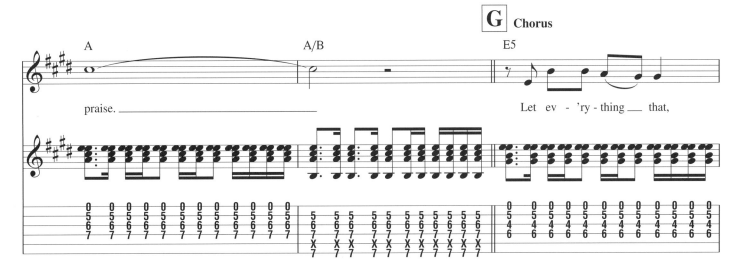

praise. _____ Let ev - 'ry - thing ___ that,

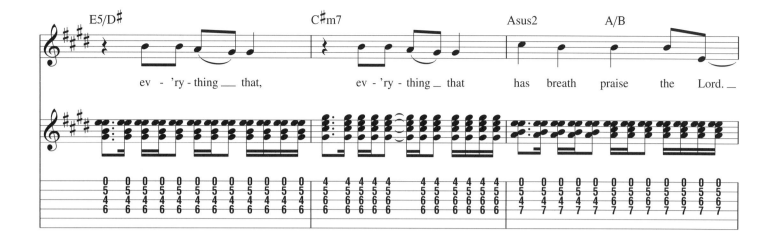

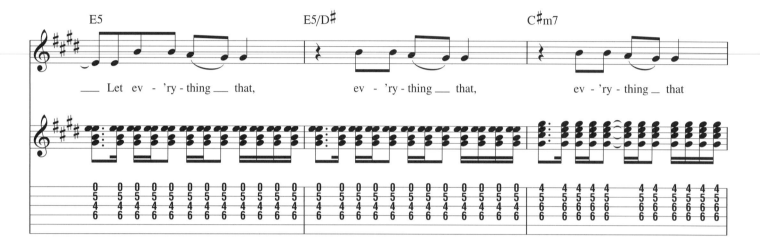

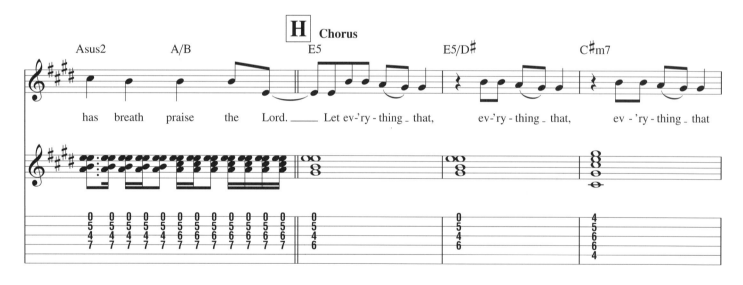

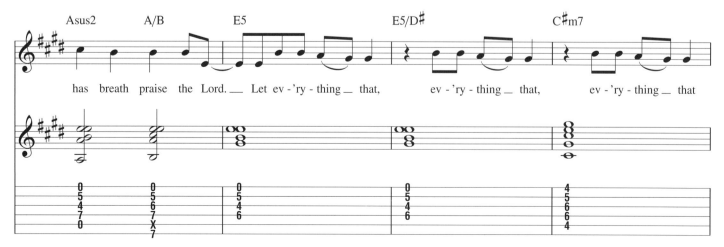

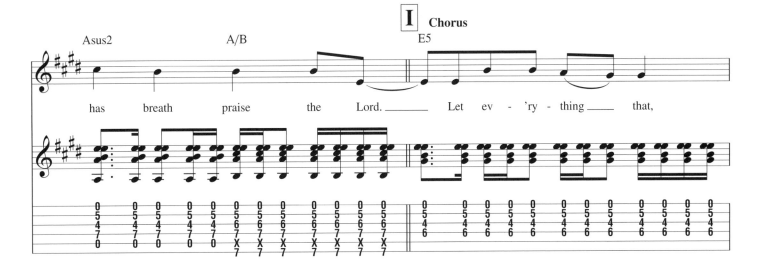

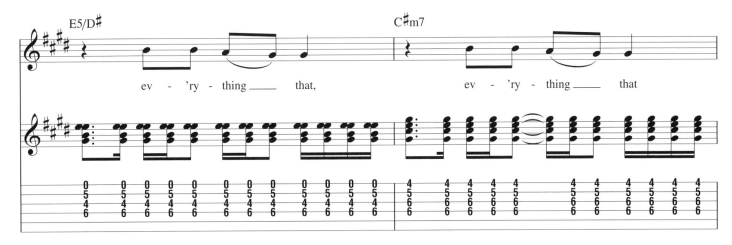

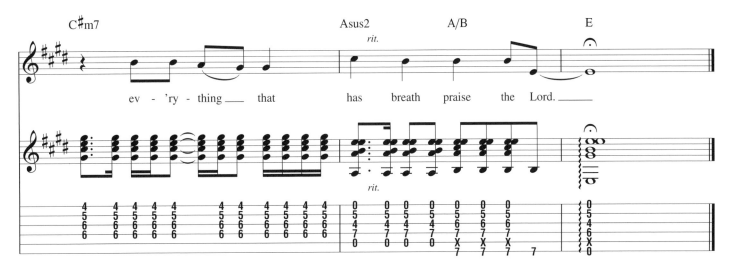

You Alone

Words and Music by Jack Parker and David Crowder

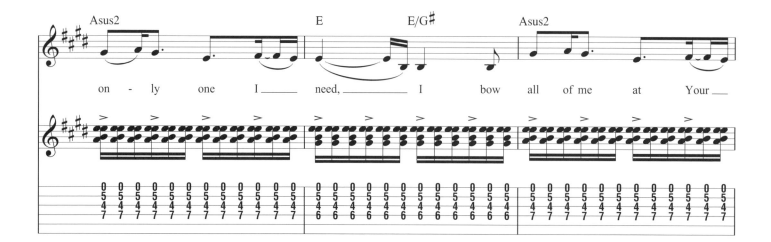

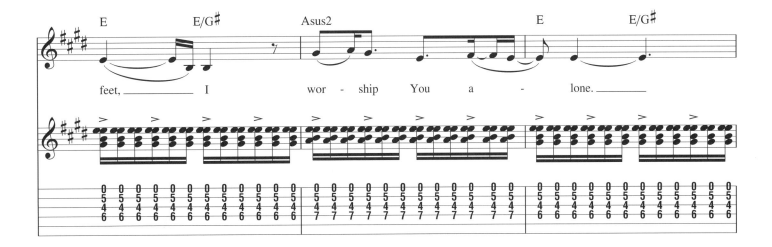

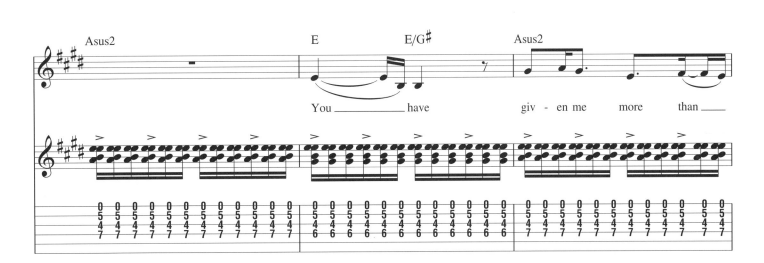

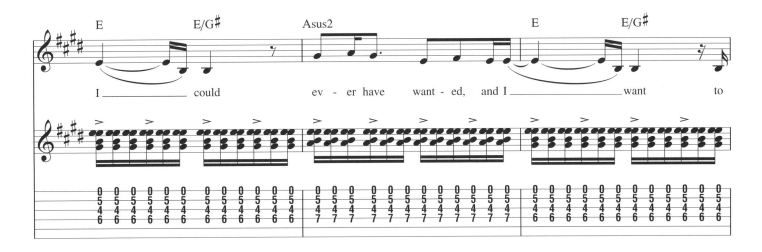

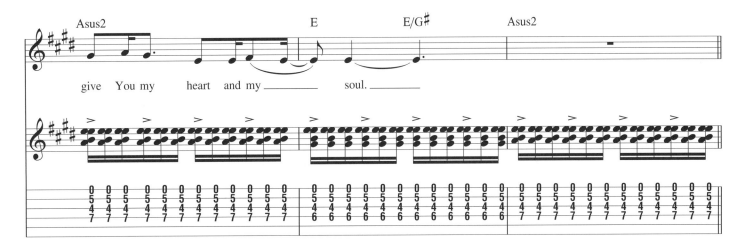

B **Chorus**

You _____ a - lone ___ are ___ Fa - ther and You _____ a - lone _

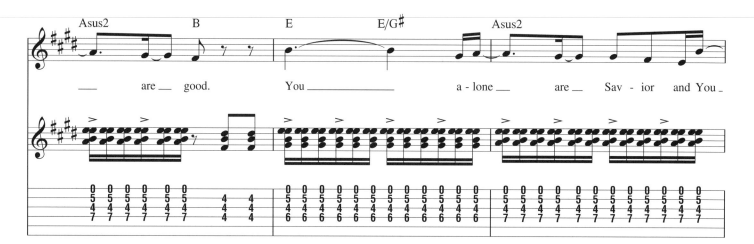

___ are ___ good. You _____ a - lone ___ are ___ Sav - ior and You _

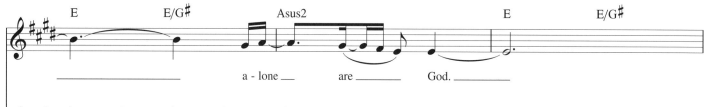

a - lone ___ are _____ God. _____

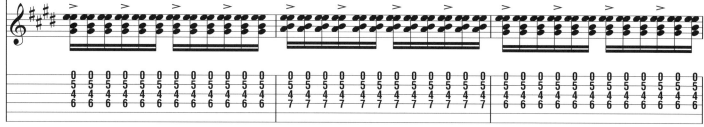

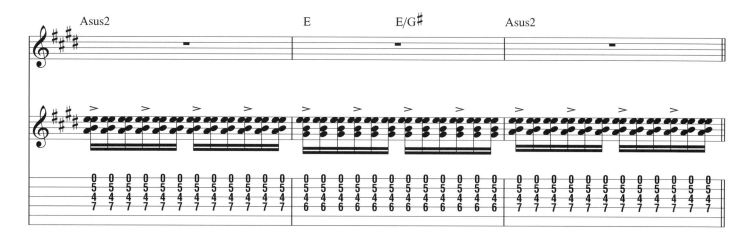

You _____ are _____ the on - ly one I _____ need, _____ I bow

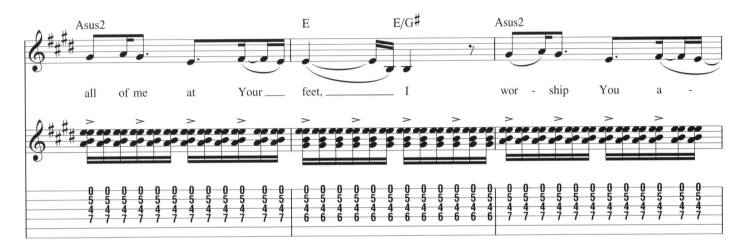

all of me at Your _____ feet, _____ I wor - ship You a -

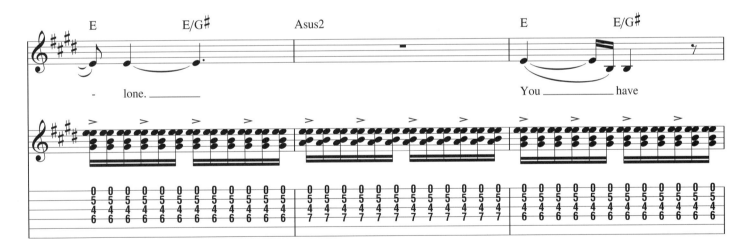

- lone. _____ You _____ have

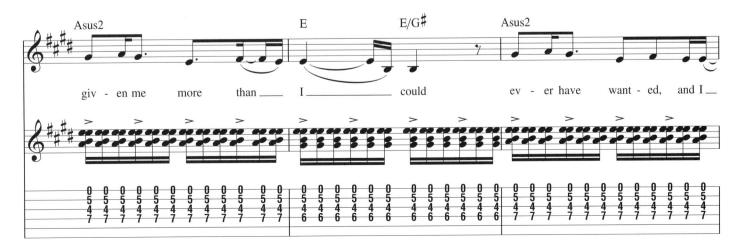

giv - en me more than _____ I _____ could ev - er have want - ed, and I _____

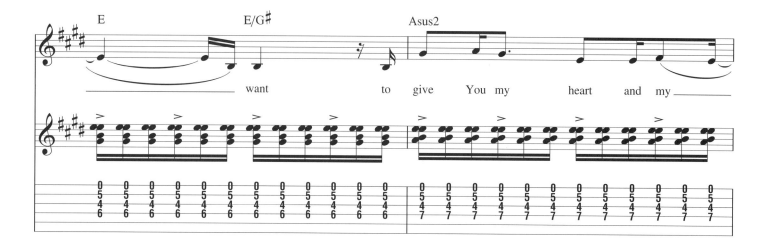

want to give You my heart and my

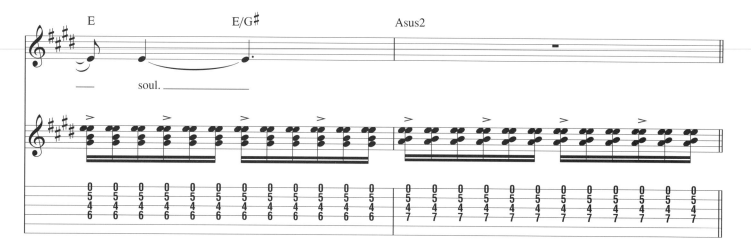

— soul. _____

D **Chorus**

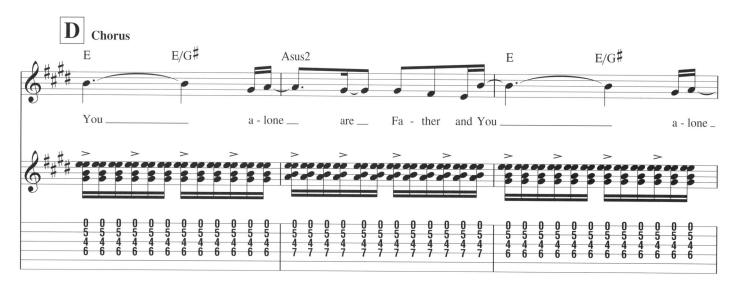

You _____ a - lone ___ are ___ Fa - ther and You _____ a - lone _

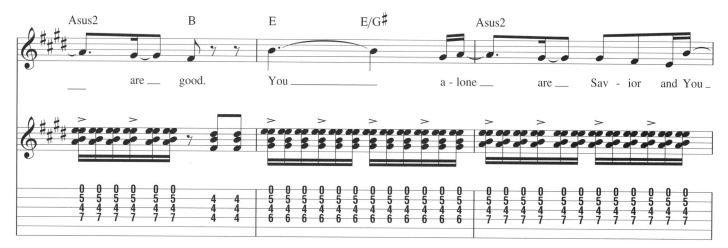

___ are ___ good. You _____ a - lone ___ are ___ Sav - ior and You _

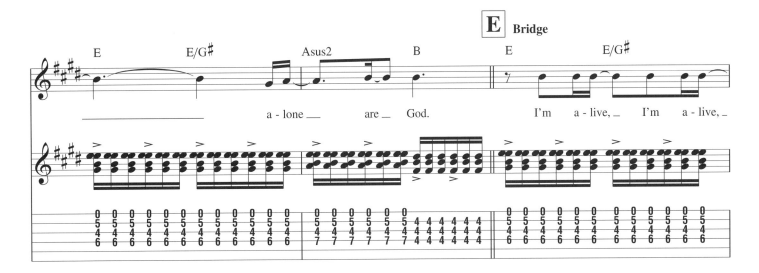

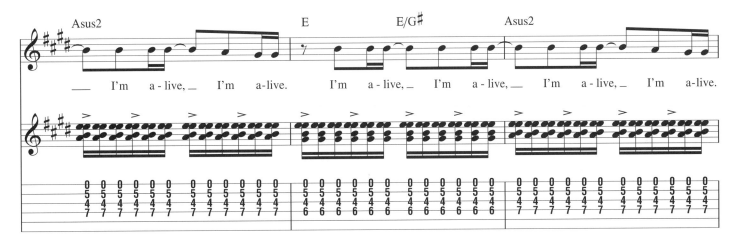

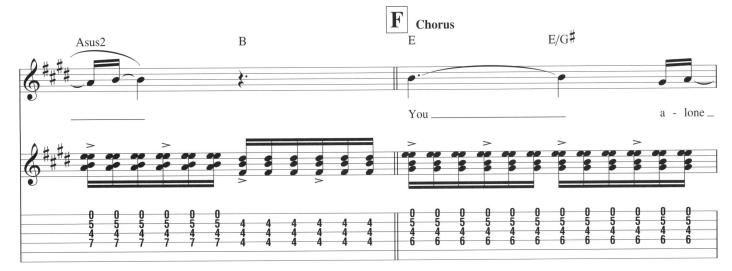

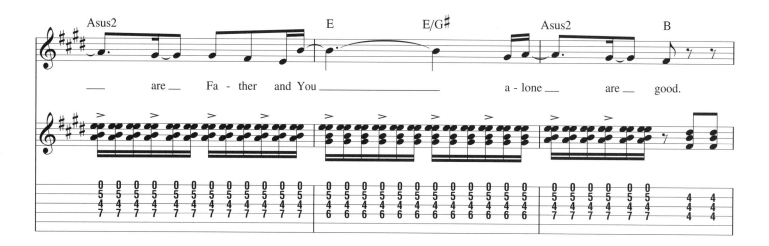

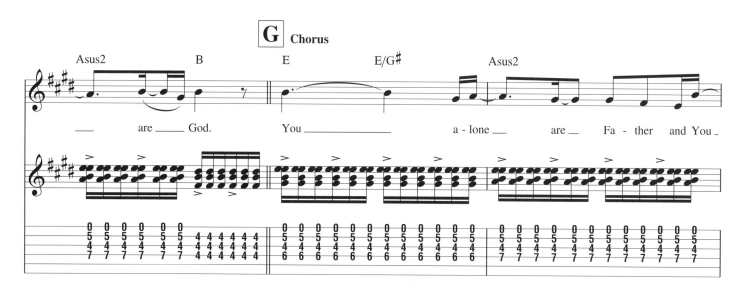

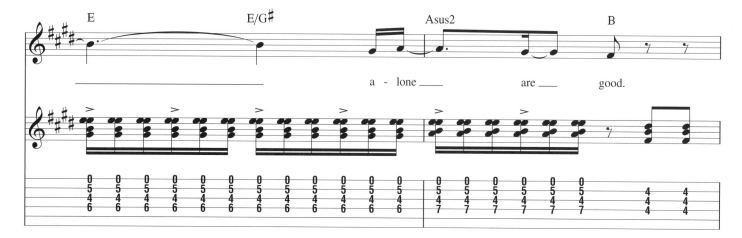

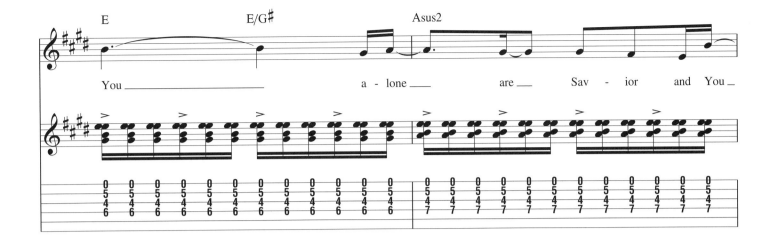

You _____ a - lone ___ are ___ Sav - ior and You _

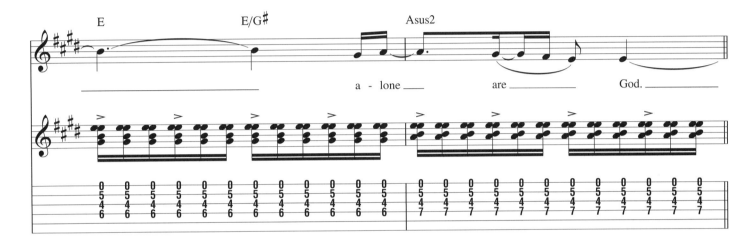

_____ a - lone ___ are _____ God. _____

Outro

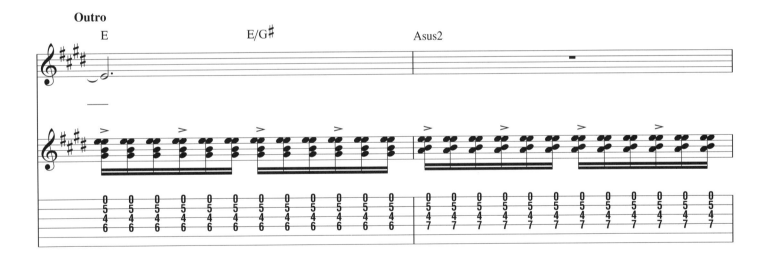

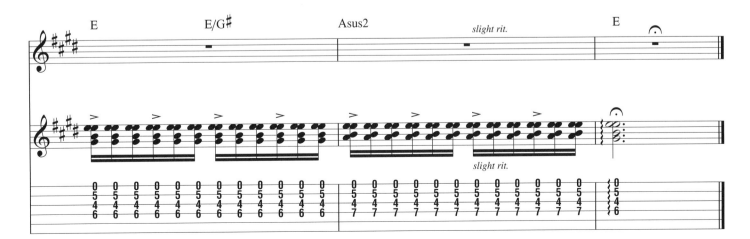

slight rit.

slight rit.

COME, NOW IS THE TIME TO WORSHIP

BRIAN DOERKSEN

Key of **D Major, 4/4**

INTRO:

D G/D D G/D

VERSE:

D   G/D   D
Come, now is the time to wor - ship

A   Em7   D/F♯   G
Come, now is the time to give   your   heart

D   G/D   D
Come, just as you are, to wor - ship

A   Em7 D/F♯ G
Come, just as you are, before   your   God

D
Come

CHORUS:

G   D
One day ev'ry tongue will confess You are God

G   D
One day ev'ry knee will bow

G   Bm
Still, the greatest treasure remains for those

     Em7   Asus   A
Who gladly choose You now

(REPEAT VERSE)

(REPEAT CHORUS 2X)

(REPEAT VERSE)

OUTRO:

  D G/D D G/D D (hold)
(Come)   Come   Come

GIVE US CLEAN HANDS

CHARLIE HALL

Key of **G Major, 4/4**

INTRO:

G   D   G/B C   G

VERSE:

G   D   G/B
   We bow our hearts, we bend our knees
C   G
   O Spirit, come make us humble
G   D   G/B
   We turn our eyes from evil things
C
   O Lord, we cast down our idols

CHORUS:

C/D   G   D
Give us clean hands, give us pure hearts
      Em   D   G
Let us not lift our souls to another
          G   D
Give us clean hands, give us pure hearts
      Em   D   G
Let us not lift our souls to another
           G   D
And God, let us be a generation that seeks
          Em   D   G
That seeks Your face, O God of Jacob
           G   D
And God, let us be a generation that seeks
        Em   D   Csus2 (2 bars)
That seeks Your face, O God of Jacob

(REPEAT VERSE & CHORUS)

TAG:

G   D   G/B
   We bow our hearts, we bend our knees
C   G (hold)
   O Spirit, come make us humble

HEAR OUR PRAISES

REUBEN MORGAN

Key of **C Major, 4/4**

INTRO:

C   Csus   C   Csus

VERSE 1:

C   Csus   C   G/B
    May our homes be filled with dancing

Am   F   Gsus   G
    May our streets be filled with joy

C   Csus   C   G/B
    May injustice bow to Jesus

Am   F   Gsus   G
    As the people turn to pray

CHORUS:

         C   G/B   F/A
From the mountain   to the valley

        Am   Em7   F   Gsus
Hear our praises   rise to You

         C   G/B   F/A
From the heavens   to the nations

        Am   Em7   F   Gsus
Hear the singing   fill the air

(REPEAT INTRO)

VERSE 2:

C   Csus   C   G/B
    May our light shine in the darkness

Am   F   Gsus   G
    As we walk before the cross

C   Csus   C   G/B
    May Your glory fill the whole earth

Am   F   Gsus   G
    As the water o'er the seas

(REPEAT CHORUS)

TRANSITION TO BRIDGE:

C (2 bars)

BRIDGE (2X):

    F   Dm7   Am   Em7
Hallelujah,   hallelujah

    F   Dm7   Gsus   G
Hallelujah,   hallelujah

(REPEAT CHORUS 2X)

OUTRO:

C   Csus   C   Csus   C (hold)

HERE I AM TO WORSHIP

TIM HUGHES

Key of **D Major, 4/4**

INTRO:

D A Em7 D A G

VERSE 1:

D   A   Em7
Light of the world, You stepped down into darkness

D   A   G
Opened my eyes, let me see

D   A   Em7
Beauty that made this heart adore You

D   A   G (2 bars)
Hope of a life spent with You

CHORUS:

               D   A
Here I am to worship, here I am to bow down

          D/F♯   G
Here I am to say that You're my God

               D   A
You're altogether lovely, altogether worthy

        D/F♯   G
Altogether wonderful to me

VERSE 2:

D   A   Em7
King of all days, oh, so highly exalted

D   A   G
Glorious in heaven above

D   A   Em7
Humbly You came to the earth You created

D   A   G (1 bar)
All for love's sake became poor

(REPEAT CHORUS)

BRIDGE (2X):

       A/C♯   D/F♯   G
And I'll never know   how much it cost

    A/C♯   D/F♯   G
To see my sin   upon that cross

(REPEAT CHORUS 2X)

TAG:

D   A   Em7
Light of the world, You stepped down into darkness

D   A   G (hold)
Opened my eyes, let me see

I GIVE YOU MY HEART

REUBEN MORGAN

Key of **D Major, 4/4**

INTRO:

Gmaj7   A/G   F#m7   Bm7

Gmaj7   A/G   F#m7   G/A

VERSE:

D   A/C#   Bm7
This is my de - sire

  G D   A
To hon - or You

Bm7   A/C#   D
Lord, with all   my   heart

    Cmaj7 G   A
I worship You

D   A/C#   Bm7
All I have with - in me

  G D A
I give You praise

Bm7 A/C# D
All that I a - dore

   Cmaj7 G   A
Is in You

CHORUS:

D   A
Lord, I give You my heart

       Em7
I give You my soul

 G/A
I live for You alone

D   A/C#
Ev'ry breath that I take

      Em7
Ev'ry moment I'm awake

  G/A   (Gmaj7   A/G   G/A)
Lord, have Your way in me

(REPEAT VERSE)

(REPEAT CHORUS 2X)

OUTRO:

Gmaj7   A/G   F#m7   Bm7

Gmaj7   A/G   F#m7   G/A   D (hold)

LET EVERYTHING THAT HAS BREATH

MATT REDMAN

Key of **E Major, 4/4**

INTRO:

E5   E5/D♯   C♯m7   Asus2 A/B

E5   E5/D♯   C♯m7   Asus2 A/B   F♯m7 (2 bars)

CHORUS:

E5   E5/D♯
Let everything that, everything that

C♯m7   Asus2   A/B
Everything that has breath praise the Lord

E5   E5/D♯
Let everything that, everything that

C♯m7   Asus2   A/B   F♯m7 (2 bars)
Everything that has breath praise the Lord

VERSE 1:

E5
Praise You in the morning

E5/D♯
Praise You in the evening

C♯m7   Asus2
Praise You when I'm young and when I'm old

E5
Praise You when I'm laughing

E5/D♯
Praise You when I'm grieving

C♯m7   Asus2
Praise You ev'ry season of the soul

PRE-CHORUS 1:

  F♯m7   E/G♯
If we could see how much You're worth

     F♯m7   E/G♯
Your pow'r, Your might, Your endless love

     F♯m7   E/G♯   A A/B
Then surely we would never cease to praise

(REPEAT CHORUS)

VERSE 2:

E5
Praise You in the heavens

E5/D♯
Joining with the angels

C♯m7   Asus2
Praising You forever and a day

E5
Praise You on the earth now

E5/D♯
Joining with creation

C♯m7   Asus2
Calling all the nations to Your praise

PRE-CHORUS 2:

  F♯m7   E/G♯
If they could see how much You're worth

     F♯m7   E/G♯
Your pow'r, Your might, Your endless love

     F♯m7   E/G♯   A A/B
Then surely they would never cease to praise

(REPEAT CHORUS 3X)

END ON E

YOU ALONE

JACK PARKER and DAVID CROWDER

Key of **E Major, 6/8**

INTRO:

E E/G♯ Asus2

E E/G♯ Asus2

VERSE:

E   E/G♯   Asus2
You   are   the only one I

E   E/G♯   Asus2
Need,   I bow all of me at Your

E   E/G♯ Asus2   E E/G♯ Asus2
Feet,   I   worship You alone

E   E/G♯   Asus2
You   have   given me more than

E E/G♯   Asus2
I could   ever have wanted, and

E E/G♯   Asus2   E E/G♯ Asus2
I want   to give You my heart and my soul

CHORUS:

E   E/G♯   Asus2
You   alone are Father

       E   E/G♯ Asus2   B
And You   alone are good

E   E/G♯ Asus2
You   alone are Savior

       E   E/G♯ Asus2   (B)
And You   alone are God

INTERLUDE:

E E/G♯ Asus2

E E/G♯ Asus2

(REPEAT VERSE & CHORUS)

BRIDGE:

E E/G♯   Asus2
I'm alive, I'm alive, I'm alive, I'm alive

E   E/G♯   Asus2
I'm alive, I'm alive, I'm alive, I'm alive

E E/G♯   Asus2
I'm alive, I'm alive, I'm alive, I'm alive

E E/G♯   Asus2 B
I'm alive, I'm alive

(REPEAT CHORUS 2X)

OUTRO:

E E/G♯ Asus2

E E/G♯ Asus2   E (hold)

YOU'RE WORTHY OF MY PRAISE

DAVID RUIS

Key of **E Major**, 4/4

INTRO:

E   D/E

VERSE 1:

E   *Echo:*
I will worship (*I will worship*)

    D/E
With all of my heart (*with all of my heart*)

A
I will praise You (*I will praise You*)

    E   F♯m7   Bsus B
With all of my strength (*all my strength*)

E
I will seek You (*I will seek You*)

D/E
All of my days (*all of my days*)

A
I will follow (*I will follow*)

E   F♯m7   Bsus B
All of Your ways (*all Your ways*)

CHORUS:

E   B
I will give You all my worship

F♯m7   A   Bsus B
I will give You all my praise

E   B
You alone I long to worship

F♯m7   A Bsus B   E   D/E
You alone are worthy of   my praise

VERSE 2:

E
I will bow down (*I will bow down*)

    D/E
And hail You as King (*and hail You as King*)

A
I will serve You (*I will serve You*)

        E   F♯m7   Bsus B
Give You ev'rything (*give You ev'rything*)

E
I will lift up (*I will lift up*)

    D/E
My eyes to Your throne (*my eyes to Your throne*)

A
I will trust You (*I will trust You*)

E   F♯m7   Bsus B
Trust You alone (*trust in You alone*)

(REPEAT CHORUS 2X)

TAG:

        A Bsus B   E   D/E
You're worthy of   my praise

        A Bsus B   E (hold)
You're worthy of   my praise

christianguitarsongbooks

from HAL•LEONARD®

ACOUSTIC GUITAR WORSHIP

30 praise song favorites arranged for guitar, including: Awesome God • Forever • I Could Sing of Your Love Forever • Lord, Reign in Me • Open the Eyes of My Heart • and more.
00699672 Solo Guitar $9.95

BEST OF STEVEN CURTIS CHAPMAN

This revised edition features 15 songs from Steven's amazing career, including: All Things New • The Change • For the Sake of the Call • The Great Adventure • His Eyes • His Strength Is Perfect • Live Out Loud • Much of You • Speechless • and more.
00702033 Easy Guitar with Notes & Tab $14.95

CHRISTIAN ACOUSTIC FAVORITES

14 hits from some of the most popular names in contemporary Christian music, such as Switchfoot, Jeremy Camp, and David Crowder*Band. Songs include: All I Need • Dare You to Move • Holy Is the Lord • My Will • No Better Place • Open the Eyes of My Heart • What If • Wholly Yours • and more.
00702237 Easy Guitar with Notes & Tab $12.95

CONTEMPORARY CHRISTIAN GUITAR CHORD SONGBOOK

Just the chords and lyrics to 80 hits from today's top CCM artists. Includes: Awesome God • Don't Look at Me • El Shaddai • Friends • The Great Divide • His Strength Is Perfect • I Will Be Here • Just One • Let Us Pray • A Maze of Grace • Oh Lord, You're Beautiful • Pray • Run to You • Speechless • Testify to Love • and more. 6 x 9.
00699564 Lyrics/Chord Symbols/Guitar Chord Diagrams.............$14.95

CONTEMPORARY CHRISTIAN FAVORITES

20 great easy guitar arrangements of contemporary Christian songs, including: El Shaddai • Friends • He Is Able • I Will Be Here • In the Name of the Lord • In Christ Alone • Love in Any Language • Open My Heart • Say the Name • Thy Word • Via Dolorosa • and more.
00702006 Easy Guitar with Notes & Tab $9.95

FAVORITE HYMNS FOR EASY GUITAR

48 hymns, including: All Hail the Power of Jesus' Name • Amazing Grace • Be Thou My Vision • Blessed Assurance • Fairest Lord Jesus • I Love to Tell the Story • In the Garden • Let Us Break Bread Together • Rock of Ages • Were You There? • When I Survey the Wondrous Cross • and more.
00702041 Easy Guitar with Notes & Tab $9.95

GOSPEL FAVORITES FOR GUITAR

An amazing collection of 49 favorites, including: Amazing Grace • Did You Stop to Pray This Morning • How Great Thou Art • The King Is Coming • My God Is Real • Nearer, My God to Thee • The Old Rugged Cross • Precious Lord, Take My Hand • Will the Circle Be Unbroken • and more.
00699374 Easy Guitar with Notes & Tab $14.95

GOSPEL GUITAR SONGBOOK

Includes notes & tab for fingerpicking and Travis picking arrangements of 15 favorites: Amazing Grace • Blessed Assurance • Do Lord • I've Got Peace Like a River • Just a Closer Walk with Thee • O Happy Day • Precious Memories • Rock of Ages • Swing Low, Sweet Chariot • There Is Power in the Blood • When the Saints Go Marching In • and more!
00695372 Guitar with Notes & Tab $9.95

THE GOSPEL SONGS BOOK

A virtual bible of more than 100 songs of faith arranged for easy guitar! This collection includes: Amazing Grace • Blessed Assurance • Church in the Wildwood • His Eye Is on the Sparrow • I Love to Tell the Story • Just a Closer Walk with Thee • The Lily of the Valley • More Than Wonderful • The Old Rugged Cross • Rock of Ages • Shall We Gather at the River? • Turn Your Radio On • Will the Circle Be Unbroken • and more.
00702157 Easy Guitar $15.95

GREATEST HYMNS FOR GUITAR

48 hymns, including: Abide with Me • Amazing Grace • Be Still My Soul • Glory to His Name • In the Garden • and more.
00702116 Easy Guitar with Notes & Tab $8.95

HAWK NELSON – LETTERS TO THE PRESIDENT

All 14 songs from the debut album by these Christian punk rockers. Includes: California • From Underneath • Letters to the President • Recess • Right Here • First Time • Like a Racecar • Long and Lonely Road • Take Me • and more.
00690778 Guitar Recorded Versions $19.95

THE HYMN BOOK

143 glorious hymns: Abide with Me • Be Thou My Vision • Come, Thou Fount of Every Blessing • Fairest Lord Jesus • Holy, Holy, Holy • Just a Closer Walk with Thee • Nearer, My God, to Thee • Rock of Ages • more. Perfect for church services, sing-alongs, bible camps and more!
00702142 Easy Guitar (no tab) $14.95

HYMN FAVORITES

60 beloved hymns, complete with chords, strum patterns, melody lines and lyrics: Amazing Grace • Battle Hymn of the Republic • Blessed Assurance • Down by the Riverside • Holy, Holy, Holy • In the Garden • Just as I Am • O Worship the King • Rock of Ages • This Is My Father's World • Wayfaring Stranger • What a Friend We Have in Jesus • and more.
00699271 Strum It Guitar (no tab) $9.95

PRAISE AND WORSHIP FOR GUITAR

45 easy arrangements, including: As the Deer • Glorify Thy Name • He Is Exalted • Holy Ground • How Excellent Is Thy Name • Majesty • Thou Art Worthy • You Are My Hiding Place • more.
00702125 Easy Guitar with Notes & Tab $9.95

RELIENT K – MMHMM

14 transcriptions from the 2004 release by these Christian punk rockers. Features: Be My Escape • Let It All Out • Life After Death and Taxes • My Girl's Ex-Boyfriend • The One I'm Waiting For • When I Go Down • Which to Bury; Us or the Hatchet? • Who I Am Hates Who I've Been • and more.
00690779 Guitar Recorded Versions $19.95

SWITCHFOOT – THE BEAUTIFUL LETDOWN

All 11 songs in transcriptions with tab from the 2003 release by these Dove Award-winning alt CCM rockers: Adding to the Noise • Ammunition • Beautiful Letdown • Dare You to Move • Gone • Meant to Live • More Than Fine • On Fire • Redemption • This Is Your Life • 24.
00690767 Guitar Recorded Versions $19.95

THIRD DAY – WHEREVER YOU ARE

This songbook features all 12 tracks from the 2005 release by this CCM band that started in Atlanta. Includes: Cry Out to Jesus • Eagles • I Can Feel It • Keep on Shinin' • Love Heals Your Heart • Rise Up • The Sun Is Shining • more.
00690825 Guitar Recorded Versions $19.95

TOP CHRISTIAN HITS

14 of today's hottest CCM hits: Blessed Be Your Name (Tree 63) • Dare You to Move (Switchfoot) • Filled with Your Glory (Starfield) • Gone (TOBYMAC) • Holy (Nichole Nordeman) • Holy Is the Lord (Chris Tomlin) • I Can Only Imagine (MercyMe) • Much of You (Steven Curtis Chapman) • and more.
00702217 Easy Guitar with Notes & Tab $12.95

TODAY'S CHRISTIAN ROCK

16 powerful contemporary Christian songs. Includes: Between You and Me (dc Talk) • Flood (Jars of Clay) • Kiss Me (Sixpence None the Richer) • Lord of the Dance (Steven Curtis Chapman) • Shine (Newsboys) • and more.
00702124 Easy Guitar with Notes & Tab $9.95

WORSHIP FAVORITES

21 songs: Above All • Ancient of Days • As the Deer • Breathe • Come, Now Is the Time to Worship • Draw Me Close • Firm Foundation • He Is Exalted • I Could Sing of Your Love Forever • Shout to the Lord • We Fall Down • You Alone • You Are My All in All • and more.
00702192 Easy Guitar with Notes & Tab $9.95

BEST OF WORSHIP TOGETHER

Includes 15 popular praise and worship songs: Forever • He Reigns • Here I Am to Worship • I Could Sing of Your Love Forever • Let Everything That Has Breath • more.
00702213 Easy Guitar with Notes & Tab $9.95

X WORSHIP 2006

15 of the most rockin' CCM hits of the year: My Glorious (Delirious?) • Spirit (Switchfoot) • I Am Understood (Relient K) • Release the Deep (Telecast) • Finding Who We Are (Kutless) • I Wait for the Lord (Jeremy Camp) • Laid to Rest (The Showdown) • and more..
00690821 Guitar Recorded Versions $19.95

Prices, contents and availability subject to change without notice.

FOR MORE INFORMATION, SEE YOUR LOCAL MUSIC DEALER,
OR WRITE TO:

HAL•LEONARD®
CORPORATION
7777 W. BLUEMOUND RD. P.O. BOX 13819 MILWAUKEE, WI 53213

www.halleonard.com

0608